KNOWING THE LOVE OF GOD

KNOWING THE LOVE OF GOD

Lessons from a Spiritual Master

Fr. Reginald Garrigou-Lagrange, OP

Augustine Institute

Greenwood Village, Colorado

Originally published under the title *The Last Writings of Reginald Garrigou-Lagrange* by New City Press, 1969. Originally translated by Raymond Smith, O.P., and Rod Gorton. In this 2015 edition, there have been minor improvements to the translation. A new foreword and introduction have also been added.

NIHIL OBSTAT: MARTINUS S. RUSHFORP, PHD.
CENSOR LIBRORUM

IMPRIMATUR: † FRANCISCUS IOANNES MUGAVERO, D.D.
EPISCOPUS BRUKLYNIENSIS
BRUKLYNI DIE 7 MAII 1969

Cover art: *Return of the Prodigal Son*
by Bartolome Esteban Murillo (1617–1682)
Museo del Prado, Madrid, Spain

Cover Design by Geoff Butz and Christopher Murphy
Layout and Design by Denise Fath

Augustine Institute
6160 S. Syracuse Way, Greenwood Village, CO 80111, (800) 777-7502

ISBN Number: 978-1-942759-00-3

Printed in the United States of America

Special Acknowledgment

Special thanks to Dr. Scott Hahn for enabling us to rescue this masterpiece from obscurity. This book would not be available without his tremendous help. Please remember Dr. Hahn, his family, and their intentions in your prayers.

Dedication

We entrust the fruitfulness of this book to the
Blessed Virgin Mary and St. Joseph.

St. Dominic and St. Thomas Aquinas, pray for us.

FOREWORD

On the day of my ordination to the holy priesthood, my seminar-ian friend Michael Hendershott gave me a book as an ordination gift. On the first page Michael wrote: "May this book by our mutual friend serve to increase charity and truth as a token of gratitude for your help in increasing these in me." The book was *The Last Writings of Reginald Garrigou-Lagrange*, and the author was the man named in the title. Fr. Reginald Garrigou-Lagrange, OP, was a French Dominican priest who lived from 1877 to 1964. A most faithful commentator on the writings of St. Thomas Aquinas and a staunch defender of the Angelic Doctor's teach-ings, Garrigou-Lagrange was one of the greatest philosophers and theologians of the 20th century. In my seminary years, the many works of Garrigou-Lagrange brilliantly illuminated my philosophical and theological studies. Michael had this same experience, and, thus, could truly call Garrigou-Lagrange "our mutual friend."

Despite my familiarity with Garrigou-Lagrange's many writings, the book Michael gave me was one I had never seen before, largely due to its having been out of print for many years. *The Last Writings* (now titled *Knowing the Love of God*) is a collection of Garrigou-Lagrange's retreat conferences as he preached them to his fellow Dominicans. Each chapter consists of one of these conferences, making this book a retreat in written form and the rich fruit of many decades of preaching, teaching, and profound prayer. Although I already had a plethora

of books on my personal reading list, *Knowing the Love of God* was
the first book I chose to read after my priestly ordination. What
I discovered therein was a precious gem of spiritual theology
put forward in an intellectually engaging and widely accessible
form. Garrigou-Lagrange is, perhaps, best known for his two-
volume masterpiece on spiritual theology, *The Three Ages of the
Interior Life: Prelude of Eternal Life*, at the end of which he offers
an outline for preaching a retreat on progress in the spiritual
life. *Knowing the Love of God* follows this outline almost exactly,
treating the spiritual life in a theologically scientific manner
which both enlightens the trained theologian and inspires the
simple soul.

In *Knowing the Love of God*, Garrigou-Lagrange treats first the
goal or aim of our spiritual life, namely, attaining supernatural
happiness with God in Heaven. Next, he speaks of sin and its
consequences as the obstacles to this goal and the impediments
to our spiritual progress. He then considers Our Lord Jesus and
His redemptive power as the source of our spiritual growth,
a growth demanding death to sin and configuration to Christ.
After discussing at length the various means for achieving this
growth, he explains, finally, the union with God attainable in this
life, a veritable foretaste of eternal beatitude.

Since reading *Knowing the Love of God*, I have been blessed to
draw from its insights not only for my own spiritual life, but
also for preaching, giving retreat talks, and providing spiritual
direction. When I offered a copy of it to Mark Middendorf,
President of Lighthouse Catholic Media, he found it so spiritually
valuable that he wanted to have it reprinted. Due to the timeless
clarity of his doctrine, Garrigou-Lagrange provides in these
pages both an enduring contribution to spiritual theology and
concrete spiritual guidance to clergy and laity alike. In an age
when the duties of daily life make it difficult, if not impossible,
for so many to spend several days away from family or work for

a retreat, *Knowing the Love of God* affords the opportunity to make that retreat from home and thereby grow in the knowledge and love of Our Lord. It is my hope and prayer that this work of spiritual wisdom, prepared on the fiftieth anniversary of Fr. Reginald Garrigou-Lagrange's passing from earthly life, will reap an abundant harvest in the hearts of many Catholics and aid them in obtaining life everlasting.

Rev. Timothy J. Draper
Holy Cross Catholic Church
Batavia, IL
Feast of St. Dominic

INTRODUCTION

The Formation of a Pope and Saint

When Catholics of the twenty-first century consider the life and legacy of St. John Paul II, they may be inclined to ask: *what type of formation and instruction contributed to this great man's spiritual legacy?* While one could list numerous significant influences, one thing is certain: St. Thomas Aquinas and those spiritual masters who studied and commented on the writings of the Angelic Doctor served as the robust foundation of John Paul II's Catholic formation.

Writing on the fiftieth anniversary of his priestly ordination, Pope John Paul II fondly remembered the "volumes of Saint Thomas with commentaries" that guided his priestly formation. "I was learning my theology, so to speak, from the 'center' of a great theological tradition." This sacred learning was not merely intellectual. Indeed, it greatly shaped his spiritual life and inspired within the seminarian Karol Wojtyla "many hours of meditation."[1]

After his ordination, love for the truth led the twenty-six-year-old priest to travel the great distance from Poland to the Pontifical Athenaeum (now University) of St. Thomas Aquinas in Rome. He explained that he enrolled at the "Angelicum" in order "to deepen my knowledge of the teaching of the Common

---

1 John Paul II, *Gift and Mystery: On the Fiftieth Anniversary of My Priestly Ordination* (New York: Doubleday, 1996), 17.

Doctor."[2] Specifically, the future Pope sought out the personal instruction of the faculty's most famous professor: Fr. Reginald Garrigou-Lagrange, OP (1877–1964).[3] Fr. Wojtyla wanted to study St. Thomas and the Thomist tradition under the wise guidance of the Angelicum's beloved "Fr. Garrigou."[4]

The Pope would later explain that his choice of mentor was not based on passing sentiment. Three decades later—a little over a year after he ascended to the Chair of St. Peter—John Paul II returned to his Roman *alma mater*. On November 17, 1979, as he revisited the Angelicum classrooms of his youth, the Pope recalled with great fondness: "Every Saturday... we came to hear the lectures of Père Garrigou-Lagrange: a great theologian, a man expert in the spiritual sciences, who at over seventy years of age kept alive a surprising vivacity!" He was a professor "who showed by his living that he was always teaching."[5] In the saint's estimation, Garrigou-Lagrange was not one teacher among many. He was a true master of the spiritual life.

Who Was Fr. Reginald Garrigou-Lagrange?

The Dominican theologian Fr. Reginald Garrigou-Lagrange was a unique blessing to the Church. Like many great men, he was revered even during his own day, suffered prejudice and neglect subsequent to his death, and has recently received renewed

---

2 John Paul II, "Perennial Philosophy of St. Thomas for the Youth of Our Times," *L'Osservatore Romano*, December 17, 1979: 6–8.

3 For more information about St. John Paul II's relationship with Fr. Garrigou-Lagrange see: Cajetan Cuddy, O.P., and Romanus Cessario, O.P., "Witness to Faith: George Weigel, Blessed John Paul II, and the Theological Life," *Nova et Vetera* 10, no. 1 (2012): 1–13.

4 For a concise summary of the Thomist tradition see Romanus Cessario, O.P., *A Short History of Thomism* (Washington, DC: The Catholic University of America Press, 2005).

5 P. Raymond Sorgia, O.P., "Record of an Unforgettable Saturday," in *John Paul II at the Angelicum* (Rome: Pontifical University of St. Thomas Aquinas, 1980), 38–39.

attention and interest.[6] While it is clear that the instruction of Fr. Garrigou-Lagrange exercised a formative role in the thought of St. John Paul II, we are led to ask: *who was Reginald Garrigou-Lagrange and what were his influences?*

Gontran-Marie Garrigou-Lagrange was born in Auch, France on February 21, 1877. The truth of God overwhelmed Garrigou while he was a young medical student. He experienced a life-changing conversion while reading a book by a French Catholic layman named Ernest Hello. "I saw in the blink of an eye that this was not a truth relative to our knowledge, but an absolute truth that will not pass away but will appear more and more radiant up until we see God face to face."[7] Garrigou-Lagrange sought entry within St. Dominic's Order of Preachers and was clothed in the black and white Dominican habit on October 10, 1897. He received the religious name "Reginald" after the famed thirteenth-century Dominican priest, Bl. Reginald of Orléans.

Br. Reginald's intellectual and spiritual mentor in the Dominican Order was the wise Fr. Ambroise Gardeil, O.P. (1859–1931). Under Gardeil's tutelage, he was introduced to the rich philosophical, theological, and spiritual legacy of St. Thomas Aquinas and the Thomist tradition. The writings of theologians like Cardinal Cajetan and John of St. Thomas helped the perennially fresh teaching of St. Thomas to come alive in the mind and heart of the Dominican student. Garrigou-Lagrange was ordained to the priesthood on September 28, 1902. Following his graduate studies, Fr. Garrigou taught philosophy and theology to his Dominican brothers in France.

---

6 For example, see: Richard Peddicord, O.P., *The Sacred Monster of Thomism: An Introduction to the Life and Legacy of Reginald Garrigou-Lagrange*, O.P. (South Bend, IN: St. Augustine's Press, 2005); Aidan Nichols, O.P., *Reason with Piety: Garrigou-Lagrange in the Service of Catholic Thought* (Ave Maria, FL: Sapientia Press, 2008).

7 See M.-Rosaire Gagnebet, "L'œuvre du P. Garrigou-Lagrange: itinéraire intellectuel et spirituel vers Dieu," *Angelicum* 42 (1965): 9–10.

His brilliance quickly attracted the attention of the Master
of the Dominican Order, Bl. Hyacinthe-Marie Cormier (1832–
1916), and in 1909 Fr. Garrigou was assigned to the Angelicum
where he would teach for half a century. He wrote over fifty
books and three hundred articles during the course of his academic career. Additionally, he served as a Consultor to the Holy
Office (now the Congregation for the Doctrine of the Faith)
and as a theological advisor to popes from Benedict XV through
St. John XXIII. He died in Rome on February 15, 1964—the
feast day of the Dominican Rhineland mystic, Bl. Henry Suso
(1300–1366). Garrigou-Lagrange lies buried in the Dominican
mausoleum in the Campo Verano Cemetery in Rome.

A Spiritual Master

While a brilliant scholar, Fr. Reginald Garrigou-Lagrange was
first and foremost a Dominican priest. Like all faithful sons
of St. Dominic, the primary intent throughout his whole life
remained the salvation of souls. Because of this zeal for the truth
of God's love, Fr. Garrigou was not an ivory tower academic.
He was a holy priest. He was known for his pastoral availability
and personal approachability. He was a true spiritual father.

His classes were imbued with life and wisdom. One of Fr.
Garrigou's former students remembered that he "was the
consummate actor in the best sense of the word... I can
compare him with the present Pope [John Paul II], with his
charismatic, even prophetic gift of effective and provocative
communication."[8] Far from a dry, boring, or aloof professor,
"in class, Garrigou's gestures, modulations, facial expressions,

---

8 Fr. Joseph De Torre, "My Personal Memories of Fr. Reginald Garrigou-
Lagrange, O.P." (Manila: 2001), 2. Though originally published as a booklet
in the Philippines, an edited version of this essay was recently included as
a chapter in the online volume: *Reginald Garrigou-Lagrange, O.P.: Teacher of
Thomism* (http://educationaltheoria.files.wordpress.com/2014/02/garrigou-
teacher-thomism.pdf).

use of the blackboard, joviality and witty humor, etc., were truly masterful." "He was famous for the rich content and brilliant delivery of his lectures."[9] Indeed, another student said that his "were probably the most fascinating lectures I have ever heard in Rome or elsewhere."[10]

One former student recalled to the present author his final meeting with Fr. Garrigou. Towards the end of an oral final exam, Fr. Garrigou looked at the then young priest and said: "Father, may I ask you a question about the sacrament of penance?" The priest was surprised because this was not a topic they had covered in the course. Nonetheless, he agreed. The elderly Dominican then asked: "How often do you go to confession?" The young priest explained that he went with great frequency. And Fr. Garrigou-Lagrange, pleased, said: "Very good: a priest can never be a good confessor without being a good penitent." This was the final thing Fr. Garrigou-Lagrange ever said to the young priest. To this day, the priest fondly recalls this final encounter with Fr. Garrigou.

A highly sought-after preacher and retreat master, Garrigou-Lagrange traveled the world during his summer vacations giving conferences and retreats to priests and religious men and women. The volume you now hold in your hands contains the conferences he gave. Reginald Garrigou-Lagrange loved his Savior, Jesus Christ. Fr. Garrigou was devoted to him whom St. Thomas Aquinas called the "wisest and best friend."[11] This love informed all of Garrigou-Lagrange's study, writing, teaching, and preaching. More than anything else, Garrigou-Lagrange loved Jesus and wanted everyone to know fully the truth of God's love.

---

9 Torre, 2.

10 Msgr. John M.T. Barton, "Garrigou-Lagrange, O.P.," *The Tablet*, February 29, 1964, 237.

11 *Summa theologiae* I-II, q. 108, art. 4, sed contra.

Knowing the Love of God was originally published in 1969 as *The Last Writings of Reginald Garrigou-Lagrange*. In many ways this was a fitting title. How appropriate that Fr. Garrigou's final published words should be collected in a book that shows—like the truth he so loved, lived, and taught—that our only end is God.

This book is a genuine treasure. It is the fruit of many years of sacred study and holy contemplation. Even over fifty years after its initial appearance, this book continues to help those known and loved by God to know and love the same God.

Rev. Cajetan Cuddy, OP
St. Joseph's Church
Greenwich Village, NY

CONTENTS

OUR THEME

AT THE OUTSET of this retreat we wish to introduce the subject of our discussions. The fundamental theme we'll be progressing in is the spiritual life. The points to be developed are *the goal*: glory and supernatural life in Heaven; *the obstacles*: evil, sin, and its consequences; *the source*: Our Lord and His redemptive work. Next, we consider the spiritual growth of charity in terms of its two great movements, *death to sin*: by means of mortification, the practice of the three vows, and the acceptance of one's cross; and *configuration to Christ*: by means of prayer, docility to the Spirit of Christ, zeal for the glory of God, and the salvation of souls, and devotion to Mary. Lastly, we treat of *union with God*.

In considering these themes may the Lord grant us a spirit of recollection, supernatural attention, sincerity, generosity, and prayer. May the Holy Spirit inspire us all with the ardent desire for perfection, grant the author the faculty of treating his subject in a manner that is not too unworthy, and enable readers to penetrate the profound sense of words repeated and heard thousands of times. Finally, may the Holy Spirit grant us the grace of total self-giving in a perfect act of charity.

CHAPTER I

The Goal: Glory and Grace

> *They are the ones He chose specially long ago and conformed to become true images of His Son, so that His Son might be the eldest of many brothers*—Romans 8:29

IN ORDER to understand what spiritual progress should be, we first must examine the end to which it tends. St. Paul expresses the idea in the text cited above, namely, a *configuration or conformity to the Word of God.* We have often been reminded of this divine doctrine but it is so sublime that we can never pretend to understand it sufficiently. Consequently, if we wish to penetrate its profound meaning we must gradually rise above ourselves. In attempting to determine our ultimate goal we shall proceed by exclusion, setting aside the lesser things that the spirit of the world proposes to us, until, after the necessary ascent, we arrive at a true formulation of our supreme end.

The Reply of the World

Why were we made? The world answers: "We were made for enjoyment, for pleasure, the pleasure of the body, the senses, the imagination, the intellect, and the heart." Enjoyment! This is to be the end, the rule, the motive of our activity. Such is the principle of paganism and every day it is becoming more and more that of the present world. At times it is a temptation for Christians also, even for us religious.

Evidently such an answer to the problem of life cannot be accepted by the unfortunate of this world who justly feel provoked to anger and exasperation. What sense does it really have for other men? This ideal or norm of life in reality makes man a slave of the events that procure or take away his pleasures; a slave of his passions and his very desires; a slave of jealousy and anger that rise within him against his own will itself; a slave of other men who can snatch away the miserable goods that form his happiness. By attempting to place himself at the center of all and to reduce all to himself, the man ruled by pleasure becomes the slave of all. He finds only disillusionment and disgust in the miserable, fleeting possessions that he has made his ultimate end. Moreover, he destroys within himself the very dignity of his manhood because, animal-like, he lives only for his body. With death he will lose everything and, what is worse, often he does not take into account the terrible punishments that await him.

Some persons have sought to live this way even in the religious life. Common life became for them a torment, the religious observances an insupportable yoke. They suffered their whole lives and, seeking pleasure everywhere, they lost their souls.

Then the world corrects its maxim and says to us: "The goal of man is an ordered and well-conceived quest for his own interests, a thing not accomplished without work, effort, and sacrifice." To acquire for oneself a position in the world! Who would dare to deny that at times this is also a temptation for us? It happens that certain religious work long years to gain a position in the community and to attain some dignity. Everything they do is subordinated to such an objective. The drive is always present and it would end up having mastery if God did not restore these religious to the right road with an opportune humiliation.

Such an attitude comes from the coldest and most arid egoism. Yet the egoist is not happy. He knows only his pleasures and personal satisfactions but has destroyed the more noble aspirations of the heart. Everyone avoids him so that his end is sad and solitary. If he thinks about another life, every hope seems denied him. He has lived only for the world and now he must leave the world.

Not even this maxim is satisfactory and so the world proposes a third: the respect of one's own dignity, that is, fulfilling one's individual and social duties. Such is the indifferent reply which stems from human pride. Man is made to develop his own intellectual and moral personality. In recent years, under the influence of Modernism we have seen this doctrine upheld even in religious circles. The passive virtues of humility, obedience and patience have been quite depreciated, while the active and social virtues that affirm personal initiative have been exalted.

This attitude contains a misapprehension. The man who pretends to love the good through the love of both his own dignity and his personal judgment concerning the good of his own personality, in reality does not love the good but rather adores himself and believes himself to be a god. If he truly loved the good he would certainly love even more than himself, and above everything else, the source of every good and of all justice, that is, the Good that is God.

Pride is always something hard and cold. The person that more or less consciously refuses to humble himself, to obey, to rise above himself to the love of God is not able to find happiness, which does not, in fact, exist in any finite good. Perhaps this person recklessly spends himself in external works both for the pleasure of spreading his ideas and of dominating. One day or other this life has to end and for those lacking charity, death appears as something absurd that comes to destroy in an instant the moral edifice constructed with the efforts of a lifetime.

The Reply of Reason

To know and to love God. The light of reason alone shows us that the ultimate end of man consists in knowing God and loving Him above all things. If we had been created in a purely natural state, with an immortal soul but without grace, our ultimate end would be precisely that of knowing and loving God. However, like the great pagan philosophers, we would have known Him only through the perfections that exist in His creatures. God would have been for us only the first cause of the universe, the supreme intellect that governs creation. We would have loved Him as the author of nature, with a love that exists between inferior and superior. There would not have been any intimacy, only admiration, respect, gratitude, without that gentle and simple familiarity that is in the souls of the sons of God. We would have been the servants not the sons of God.

Such a natural ultimate end is in itself something sublime, and could be pursued and possessed by all. Furthermore, the possession of God on the part of one would neither impede another's possession nor generate the least jealousy. It consists of a knowledge that cannot produce satiety, in a love that cannot exhaust the heart. This natural knowledge of God would leave unanswered many mysteries concerning the manner in which the divine perfections are interrelated, for example, the most inexorable justice with the most gentle mercy. The human intellect could do nothing less than exclaim: "Oh! If only I could see this God, source of all truth and goodness! If only it were given to me to contemplate this flaming sun from which the life of creation comes, the light of intelligence, and the energy of the will!"

The Answer of Revelation

Our true end, according to revelation, is to know God as He knows Himself, to see Him face to face as He sees Himself, directly and not through creatures. God was in no way obliged to grant us participation in His intimate life but He could do so and through pure mercy wished to do so.

"We teach," says St. Paul, "what Scripture calls: 'the things that no eye has seen and no ear has heard, things beyond the mind of man, all that God has prepared for those who love Him' " (1 Cor. 2:9). What the great men of this world and the masters of human wisdom have not known, "these are the very things that God has revealed to us through the Spirit, for the Spirit reaches the depths of everything, even the depths of God" (1 Cor. 2:10). St. John writes: "And eternal life is this: to know You, the only true God" (Jn. 17:3), and "My dear people, we are already the children of God but what we are to be in the future has not yet been revealed; all we know is, that when it is revealed we shall be like Him because we shall see Him as He really is" (1 Jn. 3:2). "For me," explains the Psalmist, "the reward of virtue is to see Your face, and, on waking, to gaze my fill on your likeness" (17:15).

This face-to-face vision of God is infinitely superior to the most sublime philosophy. We are destined to contemplate all the divine perfections, concentrated and harmonized in their first principle, to understand how one and the same love gives life to the most gentle mercy and the most inflexible justice, thus uniting in itself seemingly opposite attributes. We are destined to see how this love is identified with pure wisdom; how it embraces nothing that is not infinitely wise, and how all wisdom is changed into love. We are called to see this love that is identified with the Supreme Good that has been loved from eternity, to see divine Wisdom that is identified with the First Truth that has always been known. We are called to contemplate this eminent simplicity of God, this absolute pureness, the epitome of all perfections.

Who will be able to tell the joy that such a vision will produce if even now we are already entranced by the reflection of God's perfections, scattered as they are in some small measure among His creatures, by the enchantment of the sensible world, by the harmony of colors and sounds, and still more by the splendor of souls as revealed in His saints?

Finally, we are called to see the infinite fruitfulness of this Divine Nature which subsists in Three Persons; to contemplate face to face the eternal generation of the Word, splendor of the Father and image of His substance (Heb. 1:3); to see the ineffable Spiration of the Holy Spirit, this torrent of spiritual flame, the mutual love of Father and Son, which, from all eternity, unites them in a most absolute reciprocal self-giving.

Such a vision will produce in us a love of God so strong, so absolute that nothing can ever destroy it nor even diminish it. It will produce a love built on admiration, respect, and gratitude, but above all on friendship, with the simplicity and familiarity that this love presupposes. Through such a love we will enjoy above all else that God is God, that He is infinitely holy, infinitely merciful, infinitely just. It is a love that will make us adhere to all the decrees of His Providence in view of His glory, urging us to subject ourselves to what pleases Him so that He may reign eternally in us. Everlasting life for us will be to know God as He knows Himself, to love Him as He loves Himself.

The Way to Glory

Looking at this more thoroughly makes evident that such a knowledge and love cannot be realized in us unless God first deifies us in a certain manner in the depths of our soul. In the natural order man is capable of intellectual knowledge and of an illumined love superior to corporal love only because he

possesses a spiritual soul. The situation is the same in the supernatural order where we are incapable of divine knowledge and
divine love unless we first receive something of the very nature
of God, unless our soul is deified in some way, that is to say,
transformed in God. The blessed in Heaven can participate in
the divine operations, in the very life of God, precisely because
they have received this nature from Him, just as a son receives
his nature from his father.

From all eternity God necessarily generates a Son similar to
Himself, the Word. He communicates to Him His nature without
dividing or multiplying it; He makes Him God of God, Light of
Light, the splendor of His substance. Purely gratuitously, He
has wished to have other sons in time, adopted sons through
a sonship that is not only moral but real since the love of God
for His creature adds a new perfection. He has loved us, and
this creative love has made us participate in the very principle
of His intimate life. "They are the ones He chose specially long
ago and intended to become true images of His Son, so that
His Son might be the eldest of many brothers," says St. Paul
(Rom. 8:29). In this is found precisely the essence of the glory
that God reserves for those He loves: "the things that no eye
has seen and no ear has heard, things beyond the mind of man,
all that God has prepared for those who love Him" (1 Cor. 2:9).

The elect will become part of the very family of God as they
enter into the circle of the Holy Trinity. In them the Father will
generate His Word; the Father and the Son will issue forth Love.
Charity will assimilate them to the Holy Spirit and meanwhile
the vision will assimilate them to the Word, who in turn will
make them similar to the Father whose expression He is. At
that time we will be able to say truly that we know and love the
Trinity that dwells in us as in a temple of glory, and we shall
be in the Trinity, at the summit of Being, Thought, and Love.

This is the glory, this is the goal to which our spiritual progress tends—configuration to the Word of God.

Fundamental Identity of the Life of Grace with the Life of Glory

The spiritual life is able to tend to such an exalted end only because it presupposes in us the seed of glory, that is, a supernatural spiritual life which is basically identified with everlasting life.

The acorn could not become an oak unless it were of the same species and had essentially the same life as the grown tree; the child could not become a man unless he already possessed a human nature, even though in an imperfect state. In the same way the Christian on earth could not become one of the blessed in Heaven unless he had previously received the divine life. To understand thoroughly the essence of the acorn, it is necessary to consider this essence in its perfect state in an oak tree. In the same way, if we wish to understand the essence of the life of grace in us, we must consider it as an embryonic form of everlasting life, as the very seed of glory, *semens gloriae*. Fundamentally, it is the same divine life but two differences are to be noted. Here below we can know God only obscurely through faith and not in the direct light of vision. Moreover, through the inconstancy of our free will we can lose supernatural life, while in Heaven it is impossible to be lost. Except for these two differences it is a question of the same divine life. The Holy Spirit already spoke through the mouth of Ezekiel (36:25–26): "I shall pour clean water over you and you will be cleansed. . .I shall give you a new heart, and put a new spirit in you." To the Samaritan woman, Jesus spoke: "But anyone who drinks the water that I shall give will never be thirsty again: the water that I shall give will turn into a spring inside him, welling up to eternal life" (Jn. 4:14). "If any man is thirsty, let him come to Me! Let the man come and drink who believes in Me! As Scripture says: From His breast shall flow fountains of living water" (Jn. 7:37–38). "Mine is not a Kingdom of this world" (Jn. 18:36); "For, you must know, the Kingdom of God is among you" (Lk. 17:21). Like the grain of mustard seed, the leaven that ferments the dough or the treasure hidden in the field, the Kingdom outwardly does not make a striking appearance. Yet the life of grace is basically identical with that in Heaven. Jesus said so.

Without doubt while on earth we cannot see God with clarity of vision and yet truly it is He whom we attain with our faith because we believe His word that already reveals to us the profundity of God. "Now instead of the spirit of the world, we have received the Spirit that comes from God, to teach us to understand the gifts that He has given us. Therefore we teach, not in the way in which philosophy is taught, but in the way that the Spirit teaches us: we teach spiritual things spiritually. An unspiritual person is one who does not accept anything of the Spirit of God: he sees it all as nonsense; it is beyond his understanding because it can only be understood by means of the Spirit" (1 Cor. 2:12–14). "Only faith can guarantee or prove the existence of unseen" (Heb. 11:1).

Certainly supernatural life, grace, can be lost but that comes from the fact that we can go astray and fail. Grace, however, the charity in us, is in itself absolutely incorruptible, like spring water that can be preserved for an indetermined period of time provided its container does not break, or like an indestructible force that would never cease working so long as the instruments it makes use of do not refuse to work. "For love is strong as Death" (Song. 8:6). Love is strong, like death, and nothing can resist it. Its ardor is the blaze of fire, the flame of Yahweh. "Love no flood can quench, no torrents drown" *(ibid,* 8:7). It triumphs over persecutions, over the most terrible tortures and the powers of hell. We too will be invincible if we allow ourselves to be penetrated by this love. No created force will be able to overcome us.

This love, then, is identical with that of Heaven. It presupposes that we have been "born not out of human stock or urge of the flesh or will of man but of God Himself" (Jn. 1:13); that we are the sons and friends of God and not merely His servants; that we participate even in this life in the very nature and infinite life of God (*cf.* 1 Pet. 1:9). We treat of an adopted yet real sonship, because the gratuitous love of God is essentially active in relation to us, making us similar to Him, just and holy in His eyes, worthy of life everlasting.

The Holy Spirit in Us

Now we can understand why revelation teaches us that in our present state the Holy Spirit dwells in us. It is certain that in Heaven the whole Trinity dwells in the soul of the blessed as in a temple of glory in which it is known and loved. On the other hand, it is not said that the Word dwells in us here below, inasmuch as He is not yet manifested to us as the Word, as the Splendor of the Father. Likewise we do not say that the Father, the Principle of the Son, dwells in us, but we do say this of the Holy Spirit, of Substantial Love. Through this Love God has made us His sons. In fact, in our present state, charity, identical with that of Heaven, assimilates us to the Holy Spirit and the Holy Spirit, principle of our charity, is as the heart of our heart, the vivifying source that renews and sanctifies our life. He consoles us in the pains of exile, continually draws us more towards the everlasting life of the Word, always conforming us more to the Son who, in turn, will assimilate us definitely to the Father in Heaven.

Consequently, the Holy Spirit dwells in us and makes us feel His presence. We perceive the Holy Spirit with an experiential knowledge wholly permeated with the love which proceeds from the gift of wisdom. The Holy Spirit is with us as friend with friend, a strong friend who never abandons us but always cares for our moral wounds, fortifying and elevating us: Comforter, Vivifier, Renewer, Sanctifier.

In this way God dwells in infants whereas He did not dwell in the greatest pagan philosophers. He delights in making His presence felt in the hearts of the most humble Christians, while He does not make Himself felt to the theologian infatuated with his abstract and speculative science.

Behold the mustard seed in us! If we only understood the gift of God! If we only understood, as St. Paul tells us (*cf.* 1 Cor. 13:2), that it is superior to the gift of prophecy, to the gift of miracles, to the science of angels! Miracles and prophecies are only signs that permit man to recognize the word of God, whereas grace, charity, makes it possible for God Himself to live in us and make us live with His love, thereby disposing us immediately to everlasting life. Since it is the principle of all merit, every work that does not proceed from it is dead, fruitless for salvation. It is the progress, the development of this seed, that we must study, already knowing the goal to which it tends. We shall begin by considering the obstacles that could compromise or completely impede its growth.

Lord, make us understand the infinite value of everlasting life which You have placed in us. Infuse in our heart a deep hatred of evil that could make us lose it. Teach us in a practical way how it ought to grow in us, that we may become like to You and merit to be called Your brothers and friends in the Kingdom of Heaven.

CHAPTER II

Sin

Yahweh loves those who repudiate evil—
Psalm 97:10

WE have seen what the ultimate end of life is, the goal of the spiritual progress of man, namely, configuration to the Word, participation in the intimate life of the only and eternal Son, in the glory of vision. Now we have to examine what separates us from this end, what not only hinders us from attaining it but hurls us into an abyss of miseries as inexpressible as the glory of which it deprives us.

The Obstacle

What diverts us from our ultimate end is sin. Fittingly we ask ourselves: do we have the divine hatred of sin? Do we try our utmost to understand that such a hatred, which has created hell, proceeds necessarily from the love owed God, and that such a hatred must be profound, intense, and without limits as is this love itself?

To hate evil requires knowing it. Yet, too often we have only a verbal and superficial knowledge of it. We teach children the following catechism definition: "Sin is disobedience to the law of God; if grave it causes death to the soul making it deserve everlasting death. All the evils of this world are nothing by comparison with a single mortal sin."

15

The world does not believe this doctrine which comes from God, does not believe that sin is the worst evil of all. For the world the true evils are diseases, tuberculosis, paralysis, infirmities of every kind, poverty, and ruin. Pride, on the contrary, is not an evil in the eyes of the world; rather, it is even necessary for attaining success. A life given over to pleasure or laziness is not an evil for those rich enough to lead this type of existence. Forgetfulness of God is not an evil. God, in fact, according to the world, is completely indifferent to our adoration and services, infinitely above our miseries. We, say the worldly, do not wish to offend God. We seek only our own pleasure. Moreover, the violence of passion and the circumstances of life excuse us from sin. In this way the world ends by denying the very existence of sin.

Does not this spirit of the world exercise its influence even on us, making us sometimes say of deliberate venial sin what the world says of mortal sin? In explaining the catechism answer it does not seem too extreme to say that mortal sin is similar to those diseases that strike the body's vital parts such as the head or the heart while venial sin is similar to the diseases that paralyze the members and organs not absolutely indispensable to life, such as the eyes and the ears.

He who commits a mortal sin separates himself totally from the principle of supernatural life which is God. He is cut off from his ultimate end, committing, as it were, suicide in the supernatural order. He who falls into venial sin impedes the action of God from exercising itself freely on him, and little by little ruins his supernatural health just as the alcoholic ruins the health of his body. Without completely abandoning the way that leads to God, we nevertheless hamper our journey and dissipate our energies by futile delays instead of going straight ahead with speed. This deliberate venial sin may be vanity, slander, lying, sloth, and sensuousness. Some religious commit such sins with extreme ease on every occasion. They have read in spiritual writers that venial sin is a worse evil than any physical evil but they have inadequately grasped its significance, forming for themselves a very superficial concept of it. Thus they feel little hatred for such evil. When they commit it they do not really repent. They fall into the malaise of lukewarmness which has many degrees. It is a kind of swamp where there is a continual meeting of the pure air descending from above and the unhealthy fumes coming from the nether world. We shall try to find the profound sense of the Lord's doctrine on sin and to hate sin as God demands by trying to understand its malice along with the seriousness of its consequences.

Malice of Sin

Sin is essentially a disobedience to the law of God. What does it mean to disobey God? Sacred Scripture teaches us that sin is foolishness, a vileness, the worst type of ingratitude, injustice, and outrage. Sin is an offense whose gravity is, in a certain sense, infinite. All this is true, saving the proportion, whether said of mortal sin or deliberate venial sin. We should ask the Lord to help us thoroughly understand this.

Sin is first of all foolishness. St. Paul does not hesitate to affirm that those the world considers wise are fools in the eyes of God. The wisdom of the world that excuses and justifies unbelief, pride, sloth, and lust is foolishness. "Because the wisdom of this world is foolishness to God" (1 Cor. 3:19). Considering that God has deigned with infinite goodness to show us the way that leads to happiness—"learn to know Me, love Me and serve Me, and you will attain life everlasting"—are we not also foolish if we refuse to follow? We were created to answer "yes" to the divine call and instead we say "no." Thus, while God wishes to draw us to Himself, we put ourselves at a distance from Him.

The worldly person rushes to his pleasures of the moment. He compares and contrasts his miserable goods with God and in practice, by his life and his manner of acting, he does not hesitate to affirm that such nonsense is worth more than God, more than His friendship and everlasting life. How many times he says: "God forbids it but I will do it anyway!" It is as if he were to say: "Sensuality is worth more than God; money, revenge, honors are worth more than He; my judgment more than His, my little capricious will more than the infinitely holy will of the Most High." We place our childish whim in opposition to the will of God and it conquers. Is this not without doubt foolishness? It is the foolishness of an instant but it can become habitual and then produce a darkening or complete blinding of the spirit. This will be such a blinding that the transient good is preferred without hesitation to the eternal good, the poisoned fruit to the bread of life, while the sinner finally loses the consciousness of doing evil. The sinners "have. . .eyes, but never see, ears, but never, hear" (Ps. 135:16–17) and "drink iniquity like water!" (Job 15:16).

A deliberate venial sin committed by a soul consecrated to God is, in its own way, foolishness, *stultitia*. The Latin word *stultitia* as used by Sacred Scripture has a meaning in the supernatural order that is opposite to that of wisdom, of the gift of wisdom, just as the word "misery" expresses the perfect antithesis of supernatural beatitude. Wisdom, in fact, judges all things in relation to God and to the salvation of souls, while foolishness judges all, even God, in relation to ourselves and what is from our baser nature, namely, the petty envies and personal ambitions, the quest for comforts and momentary satisfactions.

A rash judgment, a hard word that wounds and separates the soul of a confrere from us is foolishness in the eyes of God and produces, without exaggeration, a momentary loss of the habit of faith just as an attack of madness results in the loss of the use of reason. Instead of seeing the soul of our neighbor in the light of faith and of the Holy Spirit dwelling within him, he is seen in a natural and merely sensible light which reveals to us an aspect of his temperament opposed to our own. Such opposition, often physical and material, becomes the supreme norm of our judgment. This is an aberration in the eyes of God which merits the name of foolishness. The natural and impassioned judgment has darkened our supernatural judgment which is the correct one, just as in an insane person the imagination takes the place of reason. We entered the convent to help build up the Mystical Body of Christ, the Heavenly Jerusalem, the city of souls, and instead we have worked to divide and ruin souls.

God has said to you: "My son, faithfully observe all of your rule, not just a part. Be submissive to your superiors who represent Me. Be humble, charitable, and I promise you sanctity, habitual prayer, a constant and indissoluble union with My Son who died for love of you, with My Son who tenderly seeks your soul and wishes your whole soul for Himself. I will make your soul His spouse, and this spiritual marriage will be so intimate that the earthly union, in comparison, will only be a symbol and a shadow." This is what God promises. Yet, we say, not with words but with deeds: "Lord, I don't want the sanctity You offer me, I don't want habitual union with Christ. Let me live in mediocrity, in triviality, in lukewarmness; it is better for me."

This is deliberate venial sin, true foolishness in the supernatural order. Such foolishness can become habitual, ending with the darkening of the spirit which induces us to see only the exterior, material, wearisome, irritating side of the exercises of religious life. Little by little it causes us to lose the understanding of the divine. The warnings that divine Providence sends us pass unobserved and like the worldly we also "have eyes and do not see, ears and do not hear," and even without being aware of it we drink in like water venial iniquity that is very real.

Sin is not only foolishness, an evil of our intelligence. It is also and above all, vileness, a profound evil of our will. Indeed, however great his blindness may be, the conscience of the sinner is aware that the act he is about to accomplish is contrary to the law of God, to his own interest, to that which is better and nobler in himself, to right reason, to the light of faith, and to charity. He gives way before the temptation and no longer troubles himself to will the good. How many times do sinners say to us, "Yes, I am well aware that I sacrifice the greater part of my time, my energies, my health, and my possessions to this blameworthy passion. My will is enfeebled and I am losing my dignity and character. I know it is foolishness but I can't do otherwise."

We also hear this reply sometimes in monasteries: "I can't do otherwise. Do you want me to be like a son under a superior who doesn't appreciate anything that I earnestly do, who doesn't like me, and who has no concern for me? I cannot! Do you want me to love as a brother this religious who has been jealous of me and has sought by all means to humiliate me? I cannot! There are repugnances that cannot be conquered."

"I cannot!" Rather we should say "I don't want to; my will is too weak." If we truly wanted to, we would pray, asking God for the grace to triumph over the obstacles that hinder us from fulfilling our duty. God could not refuse us this grace because it is absolutely impossible that God would refuse us what is necessary for our salvation. "I cannot!" To what purpose then is Communion, absolution, and the example of the saints?

I conclude with the most absolute certainty that we can but we do not want to by reason of our cowardice. The pusillanimous fear the light, they seek the darkness. In fact, their cowardice itself increases the darkness. The lukewarm religious does not want to grasp the greatness of the religious ideal because he does not want to carry it out. "He refused to understand that he should live right."

Sin is not only a foolishness and vileness, but considered in relation to God it is also the blackest ingratitude, the greatest injustice, and the gravest outrage. God is a father who has given us all: existence, life, intelligence, a conscience to distinguish good from evil, a will to choose the good, and a heart to love it. To show us His love He gave us His Son, who died for us on the Cross; He restored us again to grace making us His friends; He has called us with a special vocation to live even here on earth in the intimacy of His love; and He calls us daily to Communion, and surrounds us with a thousand interior graces. Instead of thanking Him, we put ourselves at a distance. We even come to the point of deliberately despising the graces He offers us, even His friendship itself. Sometimes we forget that we have received all from Him. Instead we boast of our intelligence and puny talents; we deliberately prefer ourselves to others; we abandon ourselves to a friendship that is based too much on feelings, thereby offending the divine friendship and saddening our adored Friend. This wound inflicted on the heart of Our Lord leaves us cold and indifferent. What kind of gratitude is this?

It is also injustice because the gifts that God gives us remain His. God, the Creator, has full rights over our life. As supreme overlord He has the right of possession over our mind and our heart, and this right, more absolute than any of our property rights, remains binding even if we forget it. He possesses this right in such an absolute manner that He would cease to be God if He renounced it. For example, He has the right to demand that we do not tell conventional lies, slander anyone, or commit even a small breach of modesty; but we wish to possess this right. All eternity would be insufficient to repair our injustice toward God.

Every injustice relative to God contains a special malice; it is an injury and an outrage. This slander and this rash judgment is an outrage towards the Holy Spirit who dwells within us; this impatient and angry word, this insubordination to our superior who is the Lord's representative is an outrage towards the Lord. In a certain sense the injury is infinite since it is raised against the infinite majesty of God, because it refuses to recognize His absolute and eternal rights, preferring a momentary satisfaction to Him. Since God is present everywhere, we outrage Him to His face, as when a son insults his mother to her face. Even more, it is not only an affront before Him but in Him that we perpetrate since it is God who sustains us and conserves us in being. We therefore turn our intelligence and our heart against Him while He continues to give us the power of thinking, living, willing and speaking.

Venial Sin

Only the saints could tell us all the evil that a deliberate venial sin contains. Yet not even they grasp all its significance, all its repercussions with respect to God, to Jesus, and to the soul.

One says venial sin, small sin, light sin. We should watch that we do not fall into this error. The smallest venial sin is a greater evil than all sufferings, all disgraces, all ruins, and all purely physical evils. All the saints affirm this. It is such a great evil that the disorder caused by venial sin, as St. Thomas says, is in a certain sense greater than the disorder generated by original sin (*cf.* II *Sent.* d. 33, a. 1 ad 2).

Certainly venial sin does not have the loss of God as its consequence. Nevertheless, it is more serious than the sin of nature in the sense that by it we act personally against God, we offend Him deliberately, thus meriting not His hatred but His anger—which makes no compromises with evil.

Foolishness, vileness, ingratitude, outrage, such is sin, whatever kind of sin, mortal or venial. What we have said should be sufficient to make us hate it, make us understand how much

God Himself detests it, and how much His infinitely delicate love is wounded by it. The sin of a religious takes on a greater seriousness and is something like the sin of the angel or that of Judas since it is committed with full knowledge.

Consequences of Venial Sin

To penetrate more fully the seriousness of venial sin, especially if it is deliberate, we must consider its consequences, that is, see all the evil it produces in our souls at the present time and what it prepares for the future, its consequences here below and after death.

In the present, in the very instant in which it is committed, venial sin deprives the soul of a precious grace. In that instant, grace was offered us to make progress in perfection, to be charitable, fervent, and industrious. If we had corresponded, our merit would have increased and for all eternity we would have contemplated God more intensely face to face. We would have loved Him more. Now this grace has been lost by our neglect, our laziness, and our limited charity.

You will say, "But I can find the moment, the occasion to gain back the good that I lost." On the contrary, the answer is "no." You will not be able to recover the quarter hour you wasted. Not even God, with all His power, would be able to restore it. This grace, a thousand times more precious than the universe, has been lost forever. It is true that the sanctifying grace in you has not been diminished, that it remains in the same degree. Venial sin, however, limits its freedom of action and can prepare its ruin.

Venial sin does not destroy charity but paralyzes its action and growth, makes it cold, and hinders its emergence. It does not kill the soul, but it leaves it without force and energy for the good. It diminishes the fervor of divine love, darkens the eyes of the soul and obscures the vision of God, just as partial paralysis without taking away life sometimes hinders considerably the body's freedom of movement.

Venial sin often deprives us of precious graces in the future. Is it that henceforth God will be less kind and less communicative? No, we are the ones who change. The graces that we refuse through our fault return to the bosom of God, or to be more exact, they are poured out again upon other souls. Our talent will be given to others who know how to bear fruit. The divine lights, therefore, become less vivid to us, the invitations of grace less frequent, less intense, and less victorious.

If today we have lost time in vain conversation, or permitted ourselves to get angry without cause, then tomorrow God will deprive us of His light at the time of prayer. The lights and energy that would have sanctified us will be taken away because of our deliberate and repeated venial faults. For example, if we deliberately and repeatedly adhere to rash judgment, our charity slowly loses its vitality. Sometimes repeated venial sins drag us indirectly into mortal sin. While the graces become more rare, the evil inclinations get the upper hand and sanctifying grace that dwells in the soul slowly loses its liberty. The intelligence is oppressed by darkness, the will debilitated, the heart hardened and we become more and more engulfed in lukewarmness. The temptations of the enemy continually become more and more serious and frequent. We become separated from a person as a result of constant rash judgments. One day or another envy and jealousy will assume such proportions that charity will suffer gravely.

"We meet in this dwelling place," says St. Teresa of Avila, "some poisonous snakes that can cause death. In these swamps there are fevers that incredibly weaken the soul and are able to cause its death." Indeed, we fall into a dangerous stupor of luke-warmness and in such a state mortal sin can surprise us. We can commit it almost without taking notice. Of the lukewarm it is written: "I know all about you: how you are neither cold nor hot. I wish you were one or the other, but since you are neither, but only lukewarm, I will spit you out of my mouth" (Rev. 3:15–16). (Concerning the lukewarmness of religious, *cf.* St. Catherine of Siena in *Dialogue*, "Tract on Obedience," chap. 162 from 1 to 5.)

Although we realize that divine mercy may hold us back on the more or less conscious descent leading to mortal sin, still, venial sin, not expiated here below, has some consequences after death that are as fearful as they are inescapable, that is, a purgatory possibly very long and terrible.

Purgatory

Purgatory is the temporary privation of the greatest good, the vision of God. It is the state of abandonment in which the soul, immersed in the darkest night, is deprived of contact with any creature whatsoever, suspended, as it were, between Heaven and earth, between the earth it has left behind and the Heaven to which it has not yet been admitted. The faculties of knowing and loving are deprived of any object, while one seeks in vain to cling to something.

The great mystics have described for us the terrible passive purifications of the senses and of the spirit through which God separates the soul from every creature, denying it every consolation, human help, and sensible devotion. He leaves the soul only the virtues, namely, faith with all its darkness, hope against every hope, and a suffering love nourished only by the very suffering that it heroically supports.

St. John of the Cross affirms that these purifications preparing the saints for the highest contemplation are more terrible than a thousand deaths. In reality, the soul without an exceptional grace would not have the strength to survive.

Purgatory will be like that. If our soul is stained with sin, it must necessarily be purified either here below or after death. We can believe that purgatory will be relatively severe for the souls that have committed only indeliberate venial sins that caught them off guard. How terrible and long will it be for the souls that sinned venially with full intent and knowledge and culpable negligence. Perhaps with their lips they never dare to say so, but their actions and life speak more openly than their mouth, crying out: "I am offending God. I know that I am wounding His love, abusing the blood of my Savior, and squandering the graces of absolution and Communion and many more. Such is the price of satisfying for an instant my egoism, my self-love, my sensuality, my vanity." What retribution will be paid in purgatory for this seductive aspect of our wretched satisfactions!

Mastery

The means of escape from this state of lukewarmness are: a good retreat; a spiritual direction that is supernatural, wise, warmhearted and energetic; a great cross; or a great humiliation that makes us return inward, showing us the things of this world and the things of eternity under the right light. A great cross can illumine our pettiness, our poverty, and our misery. Finally there is prayer. The lukewarm, impoverished, despoiled soul always has the grace to pray. Only the damned are deprived of this. "Do not harden your hearts!" Jesus calls to us all: "Come to Me, all you who labor and are overburdened, and I will give you rest" (Mt. 11:28). Our Lord has such a desire to pardon! He revealed this to St. Jerome: "Jerome, give Me your sins that I may pardon you." Yet, "many are called, but few are chosen" (Mt. 22:14) because not all pass through the narrow gate (Mt. 7:13). (See St. Catherine of Siena, *Dialogue*, "Means to Escape from Lukewarmness," 1, chap. 162; and *The Imitation of Christ*, "Corruption of Nature," III, chap. 55).

If we have the good fortune of being fervent, we should pray ardently for the lukewarm souls who habitually pray little and so badly. We should beseech Jesus not to permit us to descend into those unhealthy regions that border on the depths, but rather to make us always penetrate farther into the fertile valleys and to elevate us little by little toward those summits to which our destiny as sons of God and as religious call us.

CHAPTER III

The Redemptive Power of Christ

I am the Way, the Truth, and the Life—
John 14:6

This is the love I mean: not our love for
God, but God's love for us when He sent
His Son to be the sacrifice that takes our
sins away—1 John 4:10

THE POWER that must support us is the redemptive action of
Christ. "This is the love I mean: not our love for God, but God's
love for us when He sent His Son to be the sacrifice that takes
our sins away." Having reflected on the goal of the spiritual life,
configuration to the Word in the light of glory, we considered
what is essentially opposed to this progress and can always
threaten and compromise it: sin. Now we will see what that
power is by which we can triumph over both sin and the inclination to evil that is the fruit of sin; that power with which we can
raise ourselves above human limitations and attain the divine
end to which Divine Providence and Mercy have destined us.

Redemptive Omnipotence

The power upon which rests the spiritual life of all souls striving
to be freed from evil and raised up to God is the redemptive
action of Christ, His ever active and efficacious love directed to
the Father and to us. He Himself told us: "As a branch cannot
bear fruit all by itself, but must remain part of the vine, neither

can you unless you remain in me. I am the vine, you are the branches" (Jn. 15:4–5). The branches can live only if they are united to the vine and receive the sap from it. "Come to Me, all of you who labor and are overburdened, and I will give you rest" (Mt. 11:28)—that is, burdened under the weight of your faults and sufferings. "And when I am lifted up from the earth, I shall draw all men to Myself" (Jn. 12:32).

Life itself teaches us that the strength of a soul in the midst of trial and temptations comes from its practical and experiential consciousness of the infinite value of Redemption, of the omnipotent efficacy of Christ's death on the Cross. In the confessional one day a poor woman was explaining to the priest the moral anguish in which she found herself. She was abandoned by her husband, her sons, and by all; she was seriously calumniated by those on whom she should have been able to rely; she was sick and tormented by hunger. The priest, seeing that he was dealing with a true Christian, said to her directly: "Our Lord suffered more than you, for love of you." That poor woman, with full conviction, exclaimed: "That's true, it's really true!" She again found her strength and was able to continue on her way.

According to the definition of the Church, the redemptive act of Christ has an infinite value and efficacy. It makes satisfaction for any guilt whatsoever, repairs fully any offense against God, even though its gravity is infinite. It satisfies for all the sins of men, and still more. It compensates for all the rebellions against God, all the apostasies, all the acts of despair and presumption, all the feelings of hatred, and all kinds of crime. It merits all graces for even the most degraded souls, provided they are not stubbornly fixed in evil. It is impossible to think of a limit to the efficacy of the redemptive act.

The redemptive omnipotence of the act of Christ, who immolated Himself upon the Cross, derives from the fact that it is a perfect act of charity performed by a divine Person; the perfect act of the Incarnate Word. It is a supernatural act of charity towards God which makes Him forget all offenses. Such an act of charity performed by the Incarnate Word attains, by reason of the divine personality of the Word, an infinite efficacy to make satisfaction, to expiate, and to merit.

The catechism teaches this doctrine to children. But do we ourselves comprehend it? Has it become for us a doctrine of life and everyday experience? It is easy to say that the act of charity of Christ attains, by reason of the divine personality, an infinite value and efficacy, but, do we seek to understand fully in our meditation and prayer this simple phrase that children know by memory yet whose profound meaning surpasses the understanding of angels?

The Personality of the Incarnate Word

The personality of the Incarnate Word. What do these words mean? Many errors on the meaning of this word, personality, circulate throughout the world. Today many talk in a pompous way about the development of their personality, but, in reality, they are developing only some natural gifts that permit them to be distinguished from other persons, gifts which make their pride grow daily. They believe that to practice renunciation and the so-called passive virtues of humility, obedience, patience, and meekness, that is, to follow Christian morality in its totality, constitutes the annihilation of one's personality.

They have never seriously meditated in prayer on what constitutes the true worth of personality and the fact that it realizes its highest development in Our Lord Jesus Christ. We shall dwell a bit on this thought and strive to raise ourselves up gradually from the ordinary display of personality to manifestations of the personality of Jesus. This is the personality which had in itself the total explanation of its redemptive power.

Personality is what distinguishes man from inferior beings such as animals, plants, and stones. In us personality is the principle of our reason and liberty, a principle that assures us independence with respect to the material world, and thanks to which we shall be able to subsist after the disintegration of our body. It is a principle that permits us to act with autonomy and freedom in our present state, enabling us to resist the attraction of merely sensible goods according to the judgment of our intelligence and the choice of our freedom.

Although all men are persons, they do not thereby have an equal personality. Many live almost exclusively under the tyranny of their senses and passions without managing to rise above the level of animal life. Their judgments and actions are not determined by their own personal conviction; rather, they accept without examination the ideas of their surroundings, their newspaper, their political party. While they refuse, in full conscience, to obey their legitimate superiors, they passively subject themselves to the prejudices of a group and they allow themselves to be enticed by the most fantastic promises. They fail to escape the attraction of the moment and, having lost control of themselves, permit themselves to be urged on like an animal, consequently falling into the power of the first one to approach them. This is the lowest level of personality.

Personality can be gradually elevated as the activity of our spirit and will free itself from the purely sensible life. This can be accomplished in the measure that we learn to control the influences exercised upon us instead of passively submitting to them. Finally, personality can be elevated insofar as we learn to decide and choose with full freedom, instead of responding instinctively to the attraction that solicits us.

In this development of personality, however, there lies a grave danger. Since personality is measured by the independence of the being who acts, some believe that the highest development of personality consists in absolute independence. They consider this independence not only in relation to the lower levels of reality, to which we must never allow ourselves to be enslaved, but also in relation to our superiors and God Himself. The true names for this false personality are insubordination, rebellion, unbelief, and atheism. It derives essentially from pride and is found fully realized in the Devil.

The mystery of the Incarnation teaches us, on the contrary, that the human personality develops in the measure that the soul, elevating itself above the merely sensible world, places itself in closer dependence on what constitutes the true life of the spirit. That means closer dependence on truth and grace, and, in the ultimate analysis, on God.

While the great philosophers scarcely caught a glimpse of this, the saints truly grasped the way to the full development of our personality. It consists in losing in some way our own personality in the personality of God who alone possesses personality in the perfect sense or the word. He alone is absolutely independent in His being and actions, that is, He alone is independent of all creation.

Hence the saints at the level of knowledge and love made strenuous efforts to substitute the personality of God for their own, to die to themselves so that God might reign in them. They were armed with a holy hatred of their own ego. They sought to make God the principle of their actions, no longer acting according to the rules of the world or their own limited judgment, but according to God's ideas and rules as received through faith. They sought to substitute the divine will for their own, and to act no longer for themselves but for God, loving Him not as themselves but infinitely more than themselves and more than any other thing whatsoever. They understood that God had to become for them another ego more intimate than their own. They had to realize that God was more "them" than they themselves because He is preeminently Being. Therefore, they made strong efforts to renounce their personality and every attitude of independence before God; they sought to make of themselves something divine. Consequently, they developed the most forceful personality conceivable. They obtained in some way what God possesses by nature, namely independence from every created thing, not only in the corporeal world but also in the world of intelligence.

"The saints have their empire, their glory, their victory, their splendor, and they have no need of carnal or spiritual splendors; knowledge of human science adds nothing to their perfection in the supernatural order. (Being a genius in mathematics adds nothing to a saint.) They are seen by God and the angels, not by men and inquiring spirits. God is sufficient for them!" (Pascal).

The saint, once he has come to substitute in some measure the personality of God for his own, can exclaim with St. Paul: "I have been crucified with Christ, and I live now not with my own life but with the life of Christ who lives in me" (Gal. 2:19–20). Is it he then who lives henceforth or is it God who lives in him? In the order of the operations of knowing and loving the saint has substituted, as it were, the divine ego for his own ego, but in the order of being his ego remains distinct from God.

In this respect Christ, the Man-God, appears as an unreachable goal to which sanctity still strives to draw near. In Him it is no longer only in the order of knowledge and love that the human ego makes room for a divine Person, but also in the order of being itself, the root of operations. One must properly say of Jesus that He has absolutely no human personality but exists and subsists entirely in the power of the very personality of the Word with which He constitutes one unique being. This, then, is the ultimate reason for this prodigious personality of whom history has never given another example and never will. Here is the ultimate reason for the infinite majesty of this unique and exceptional ego that belongs to Christ.

"The Father and I are one" (Jn. 10:30). "I am the Way, the Truth and the Life" (Jn. 14:6). "Come to Me, all you who labor and are overburdened, and I will give you rest" (Mt. 11:28). I shall pour new strength into your weary souls and I shall raise up your dead souls. "If any man is thirsty, let him come to Me! Let the man come and drink who believes in Me! As Scripture says: From his breast shall flow fountains of living water" (Jn. 7:37–38). "Everyone who believes has eternal life. . . .And I will raise him up at the last day" (Jn. 6:47, 44). "Anyone who prefers father or mother to Me is not worthy of Me" (Mt. 10:37).

This ego of Christ is the ego of the Incarnate Word. Just as in us the soul and the body belong to the same person, so in Him the humanity and the divinity belong to the same person, that of the Word.

The Charity of Christ

What then will be the value of an act of charity of Christ if already an act of charity performed by the most humble Christian is superior to the intuitions of a genius, and if an act of charity performed by the saints produces such great wonders in the souls of those around them! What will be the value of an act of charity of Christ, an act of the human will that belongs to the Word! The smallest act of charity of Christ is sufficient to redeem humanity and repair all rebellions because the smallest meritorious act of the Word has an infinite value.

We know what this act of charity of Jesus was. It is already true that "a man can have no greater love than to lay down his life for his friends" (Jn. 15:13). But Our Lord has given His life for His enemies and for those of His Father. At Gethsemane He saw all the past and future sins including those of His executioners; He saw His abandonment by His own followers, the persecutions, the apostasies, and the hatreds; He saw the infinite gravity of the offense to God. In His human soul He suffered for all the evil and all the insults made to God His Father in proportion to His love for Him and for us. He suffered in the way an older brother suffers when he sees his father offended by younger brothers whom the father had always tried to lead to the good.

Jesus took upon Himself the responsibility for all the sins of men, and He began to suffer for them as if it had been He who had committed them, as if He were impious, rebellious, frenzied, cowardly, ungrateful, and sacrilegious. He felt the divine anger and divine curse weigh on His soul while hell with supreme fury broke loose against Him. The horror of evil and all vices together seemed for an instant to suffocate Him. A cry burst from His lips on the Cross: "My God, My God, why have You deserted Me?" (Mt. 27:46).

In this darkness, in this abandonment, Our Lord performed His greatest act of love. In the midst of this anguish He loved His Father above everything and He loved us even to the giving of His life for our salvation, only grieving that a greater number were not saved. This act of love makes abundant satisfaction for all hatreds. The obedience that it involves compensates for all rebellions in the eyes of God. The humiliations of the Passion redeem all acts of pride. The gentleness of Him crucified repairs all acts of anger and His sufferings pay for all sensuality.

The Mystical Body

This act of charity of the Incarnate Word has saved the world. This act can still save us today and sustain all souls. "Christ, as we know, having been raised from the dead will never die again" (Rom. 6:9), "since He is living forever to intercede for all who come to God through Him" (Heb. 7:25). His act of love continues to defend us against all the seductions of the world and the Devil.

Who can doubt the infinite efficacy of the love of Christ and His omnipotence against evil? "With God on our side who can be against us?" (Rom. 8:13). "Nothing therefore can come between us and the love of Christ, even if we are troubled or worried, or being persecuted, or lacking food or clothes, or being threatened or even attacked. . . .For I am certain of this: neither death nor life, no angel, no prince, nothing that exists, nothing still to come, not any power, or height or depth, nor any created thing, can ever come between us and the love of God made visible in Christ Jesus Our Lord" (Rom. 8:35–39).

This redemptive work of Christ eagerly awaits being poured out abundantly over us. Christ is the head of humanity and the life of grace flows from Him into mankind in the same way as in the human body the stimulus of the nerves is transmitted from the head to the members, and in the tree the sap flows from the trunk into the branches. The souls united to Christ through faith and charity form, in fact, a body that is aptly called "The Mystical Body" of Christ. It is a reality more genuine than the human body. Just as the life of the spirit is greater and more real than the life of the senses, which is, as it were, only a shadow of the former, so, in its turn and to a greater extent, the supernatural life is more true and more real than the human body or even the natural life of the pure spirit.

The bonds that unite the members of the Mystical Body to one another and to Jesus Christ are consequently the supernatural bonds of a reality so eminent that only God can accomplish it and completely understand it.

The principal act of the Mystical Body of the Lord is the oblation of the sacrifice of the Mass. The priest offers the sacrifice in the name of the faithful, but it is principally Christ Who offers Himself through the priest. It is always the same and unique oblation of the sacrifice of the Cross that is repeated in unbloody form, an act ever alive in the heart of Christ who does not cease interceding and offering Himself to His Father for us. I would even say, under this aspect, that Christ continues to suffer for us, as the devotion to the Sacred Heart says, to suffer in His members and in His saints, as a mother suffers in her son when she sees him in pain. The sacrifice of the Cross continues, then, in a mysterious but real way in the sacrifice of the Mass, and it is this act of oblation of the Son to His Father that sustains the world.

Life is poured out into the Mystical Body by means of the sacraments: by means of absolution that raises the dead members to life; through the Eucharist that conserves the life of grace and renews the fervor that venial sin has weakened; and finally by means of all the interior inspirations and all the actual graces with which the Lord favors us. It is a fountain of divine life that flows from Him to us, streaming forth into everlasting life. How many times we have noticed this power of Christ: in our individual lives, through absolution and Communion; and in the social life of the Church, always rising from the worst persecutions younger and stronger!

Hence, we should have confidence in this redemptive power of Christ on which the whole supernatural life must be founded. We should listen to His invitation: "Come to Me. . .and I will give you rest." "In baptism I gave you a pure and shining soul," He seems to say to us, "and see how spoiled is the one you have; but, come to Me and I shall refashion it. Come to Me, all you who have darkened your intelligence and lost sight of the ideal, and I shall enlighten you. Come to Me, you who have a conscience that has gone astray and I shall set it straight. Come to Me, you who have a weak will, and I shall strengthen it for you; and you who have a stubborn heart, come and I shall teach it anew the joy and love of God."

Jesus Christ has the power to lead us to our ultimate end and He alone can configure us to the Word of God because He is the Word. Knowing our sins, He wishes not only to heal us but through His blood to raise us up higher. "However great the number of sins committed, grace was even greater" (Rom. 5:21).

In His revelations to St. Margaret Mary He laments the coldness of some souls consecrated to Him. We should permit Him to work in us, allow Him to assimilate us to Himself, and ask Him to teach us in a practical way to cooperate with His action and to travel the way that He Himself has outlined for us.

CHAPTER IV

The Love of God

We are to love, then, because God loved us first—1 John 4:19

WE have examined what the aim of the spiritual life is, what obstacles oppose it, and what is the divine power upon which it is based. Now we shall consider what our cooperation with the action of God ought to be, what the spiritual life is, and what the general laws are that regulate its development. Reason and faith describe this for us.

The First Commandment

Our cooperation requires conforming our will to that of God and observing His commandments. The first of these, the beginning and end of all the others (to which also all the counsels of the religious life are subordinated), consists in the love of God: "You shall love Yahweh your God with all your heart, with all your soul, with all your strength" (Deut. 6:5).

Charity is called the bond of perfection, *vinculum perfectionis* (*cf.* Col. 3:14), because it unites our soul to God, our ultimate end, and makes all our forces and all our actions converge toward Him. Since it must lead us to our ultimate end, it must command all the other virtues, subordinating them to this end.

"It is the principle as well as general of the army of virtues," says St. Francis de Sales, "and to it we must attribute all the deeds through which we attain victory."

Hence, without charity we are nothing: "If I have all the eloquence of men or of angels. . .if I have the gift of prophecy, understanding all the mysteries there are, and knowing everything, and if I have faith in all its fullness, to move mountains, but without love, then I am nothing at all" (1 Cor. 13:1–3). Without charity our will is not conformed to that of God, while charity, true charity, suffices for all because it embraces all the other virtues which are subordinate to it. In this sense St. Augustine could say: "Love, and do what you wish." If you really love, what you do will be good.

We ought to meditate upon the nature of charity and see how this supernatural love of God can become the principle of our whole life and can set us on the way to glory, to configuration to the Word, and to perfect possession of God.

Natural Love, Supernatural Love

Natural reason and experience can tell us what love is not; only faith can reveal to us what it is. Ordinary reason and experience show us that our hearts here below are unable to find anything that can fully satisfy them. When we believe that we have found happiness in a created good, in a position that we have desired for a long time, in a new science, in a very intimate and elevated friendship, very soon we realize that it is a case of a limited good and, therefore, insufficient for a nature like ours that can conceive of an unlimited, total, absolute good which it naturally desires.

The profound boredom which worldly persons experience and drag with themselves to every part of the world is a sign that their heart was made for a good infinitely higher than anything they are seeking. The continual need of change that pushes them first toward one creature and then another, each of which they abandon in turn after having enjoyed its pleasure, is a sign that God alone can fill the infinite emptiness of their hearts.

According to a rigorous philosophic principle, our will possesses an infinite profundity, so that finite goods, incapable of reaching to its depths, are hardly even able to skim its surface. God alone can satisfy our needs and give us that fountain of living water about which Our Lord spoke to the Samaritan woman and which alone can truly quench our thirst. For this reason St. Catherine of Siena says to us: "Do you want a friendship that will be lasting? Do you wish to quench your thirst continually from this cup? Let it always be filled at the fountain of living water; otherwise you will soon empty it and it will no longer be able to satisfy your thirst."

Common reason and experience show us the possibility and necessity of loving God. They even tell us that this love ought to be the principle of every human life, just as the love of art is the principle of the artist's life, as love of science is the principle of the scientist's life, as love of country is the principle of the soldier's life, of his hard labor and of the sacrifices that he imposes on himself. But love of art, science, and country is not sufficient to satisfy the heart of man, who can conceive of the absolute good, aspire to it, and feel that he should subordinate his whole life to it.

Consequently there is a natural love of God which reason by itself can teach us and which was also extolled by the great pagan philosophers. But this natural love of God is infinitely far from Christian charity which is essentially supernatural. Supernatural love is a love of friendship for God which ordinary reason cannot grasp.

In fact, the spiritualistic philosophers, outside Christianity, do not hesitate to affirm that they are indeed able to have feelings of ideal admiration, gratitude, and respect for God. Yet, according to them it is impossible to love with a love of friendship a being whom we have never seen, a being so superior that He is by Hs nature invisible and incomprehensible, a being to whom we owe all things but for whom we can do nothing. Friendship presupposes that the person who is loved is seen. Furthermore, it demands a certain equality, a certain common life, the reciprocal revealing of one's most intimate thoughts and the possibility of one doing good for the other. Between God and us such a love of friendship cannot be realized. So speaks reason left to itself.

Revelation. What reason cannot discover, Christ has revealed to us. St. Paul says that He has shown us God's excess of love for us and taught us that our love ought to be a response and be modeled on the very love God has for us. "We are to love, then, because God loved us first" (1 Jn. 4:19). We must meditate together on what God's love for us has been, on what has been the response of the saints, and on what our response should be.

The Love of God for Us

God's love for us is said to be excessive and foolish. St. Paul defines God's love for us as an "excess" since it infinitely exceeds and surpasses what reason can comprehend and the heart can desire. Relative to us, it is excessive but not in itself. St. Paul also calls it, and without exaggeration, "foolishness" because this love has in some way overturned the natural relationship of God toward the creature. In Christ He died in place of the creature who had become His enemy. Such a thing is inconceivable foolishness for natural reason. Aptly then is it defined as "the foolishness of the Cross" and such "foolishness" is reparation for that other foolishness which is sin.

We should meditate upon this excess of love. True love whereby another being is loved, not only for one's own self-interest but for the other being itself, is not only a passive love but is also active. It is not a simple emotional satisfaction that is born at the sight of a pleasing object, but rather an effective and operating love whereby the good of the loved person is willed.

This active love consists in going outside of self and one's own egoism to be carried toward the being whose good is willed; in uniting oneself to this being by a communion of will and sentiment; and in dedicating oneself to the other being, in giving oneself to it in order to elevate it, make it better and more beautiful.

Hence, the mother bends over her baby, forgetting about herself and all her preoccupations, to dedicate herself entirely to this little being who lives solely because of her. Then she takes him, embraces him, presses him to herself as if she wished to form one single being with him. She dedicates herself to him, day and night, and she gives him food of body and soul that he may grow and become gradually opened to the life of reason and grace.

This type of true love enables us to catch a glimpse of what has been God's excess of love for us. The charity of God for us is a love essentially active and effective. How could it be simple emotional satisfaction since all that God finds pleasing in us comes from Him and cannot be given to us except through gratuitous love? The love of God, far from supposing lovableness in those it loves, creates it in them through pure benevolence.

God has no need of us. He was infinitely happy without us because He Himself is the infinite good. He created us through pure benevolent love and through pure love He gives us at every moment all that is necessary for our physical, intellectual, and moral life. His love for us goes beyond the exigencies of human nature and anything it could conceive and desire, elevating it to the supernatural order, allowing it to participate through grace in His intimate life.

Yet, man did not know how to worthily appraise the infinite value of this divine life. In his blindness he undervalued it, even to the point of sinfully preferring an infinitely inferior

life. Therefore, through his own fault he fell headlong from the
supernatural heights to which divine mercy had elevated him.

But see how God's love comes to look for man even in his
ruin and misery. It is here that this foolishness, which overturns
in a certain sense the natural existing relationship between the
Creator and His creature, begins.

We were fallen, but God wished to stoop down over us, to
descend to our level, just as a mother stoops down toward her
baby. He was divested of His glory, of His infinite majesty. He did
not wish to appear in the natural splendor of His magnificence
as upon Sinai. He wished, as it were, to make Himself nothing.
As St. Paul says, "He emptied Himself" to bring Himself down
to our level. He took a body and a soul like ours, divesting
Himself of all glory and choosing the most humble condition
among men. He wished to be born the son of a laborer and to
place Himself in the number of the poorest so that all might be
able to come to Him without fear.

In abasing Himself and uniting Himself to us by assuming
our nature, God wished to share in our life itself. Consequently,
He fulfilled our duties, suffered our pains, experienced our
weariness, perspired with our sweat, shed our tears, embraced
us and desired our happiness more than we can ourselves. Even
more, the Word of God wished to wash our feet.

Finally, He desired to accomplish the total gift of self by
dying on the Cross for us. After having undergone the worst
humiliations, He shed His blood in the midst of atrocious
sufferings. This He did to restore our inheritance and make us,
in some way, equal to Himself. He elevated us to the order of
the supernatural, divine, and eternal life which in our blindness
we had despised and lost.

Yes, St. Paul can speak of an "excess of love" because the
natural relationships between the Creator and the creature are
exceeded. He can speak of "foolishness" since the natural

relationships of the Creator toward His creature are, in a certain sense, reversed. God, offended, dies for the culpable creature who despises and flees from Him! Something of this "foolishness" can be glimpsed from the example of certain Christian mothers who, in the excess of their love, offer themselves as victims for a son who insults and dishonors them.

The rationalists are not wrong in saying that reason, left to itself, cannot comprehend. In fact, one is dealing with a foolishness that nature cannot conceive, which to the rationalists seems unworthy of God. One is dealing with an abyss of supernatural love in which reason is lost; only faith can admit it, only the gaze of the saints can penetrate it. Yet, only in Heaven by the light of the Beatific Vision will the infinitely superior harmony of this mystery ever be completely unveiled.

But the light of faith is still not wholly sufficient. The light of experience and of vision are necessary. Theology itself, with the light of faith alone cannot demonstrate the expediency of the Cross. Theology is hardly able to attempt an interpretation of certain exclamations of Our Lord as: "My God, My God, why have You forsaken Me?" (Mk. 15:34, Mt. 27:46).

Our Lord has loved us still more, if such can be said. Indeed, at the moment He left us and deprived us of His sensible presence He declared His wish of remaining with us even to the end of time and of giving Himself to us in a more intimate and complete way. It was not sufficient for Him to have abased Himself to the level of the Incarnation; He wished to abase Himself even to the level of the Eucharist, to empty Himself to the point of disappearing under the appearances of bread and wine. Although He foresaw in the smallest details all the profanations that would take place, He chose to remain just as docile in the hands of the sacrilegious priest as in the hands of the saintly priest. It was not sufficient for Him to unite Himself to us to become our life; He wished also to unite Himself to us, to each of us, body and soul, in Communion. It was not sufficient to shed His blood for us; He wished to give us His body for food, He wished to be eaten by us that He might be able to transform and assimilate us still more to Himself. Such is the excess of God's love for us, but this love demands a response.

The Response of the Saints

The response that the saints have given is this. They have done their utmost to love God with a love identical to His. God's love is a love that is essentially active and effective, a love that acts and creates. The saints were not content with a simple emotional satisfaction, with a wonderful admiration, or with that superficial enthusiasm that is born from the idea of the divine perfections. They understood the saying of Jesus: "It is not those who say to me, 'Lord, Lord', who will enter the Kingdom of Heaven, but the person who does the will of My Father in Heaven" (Mt. 7:21). They did not measure their charity on the basis of the sweetness of sensible devotion; instead, they loved God with a profound love of the will, which subsists even in the midst of desolations and aridity. This is a profound love which is nourished, as St. Catherine of Siena says, not only from the milk of spiritual consolations but also from the hard bread of tribulations. Here was love through which they desired first and foremost the glory of God and His Kingdom. The saints were consumed with a thirst for justice and the Kingdom of God.

The love of the operating will endeavored to reproduce in its entirety the love of God. God had stooped down toward us, in the excess of His love, abasing Himself even to our level; He had descended quite lower than we, even to the point of taking upon Himself the gravest humiliations. The saints understood that they, in their turn, should humble themselves before God, because God had reversed His role. They wanted to humble themselves, to descend from the throne of their own self-love, and to seek the last place and that obligation of service that God had chosen for Himself on earth.

We have seen a king like St. Louis kneel with his forehead in the dust before the gates of the cities of Palestine and beseech God not to permit a curse to fall on those cities because of sins. We have seen some saints, such as St. Benedict Labre, take as much care to remain with those who insulted him as he did in fleeing those who praised him.

Just as God emptied Himself and renounced His glory in order to live our life, so the saints wished to die to the purely natural life of senses, of self-love and egoism, to allow themselves to be penetrated by divine life. Just as the higher a building is to be raised, so much deeper the foundation must be, they understood that the more abundantly divine grace was to fill them, so much the deeper the selflessness that humility had to hollow out in them.

After being so humiliated the saints attained the deepest union with God. Just as God had willed to take a human way of acting, so they willed to acquire a divine way of acting. They retired into solitude to live in continual recollection. When they were unable to separate themselves physically from the world, they constructed for themselves, as St. Catherine of Siena did, a cell in the most intimate part of their heart, to live there in constant union with God.

Who can tell us what the object of love was for St. Dominic or St. Thomas Aquinas in those nights of penance and prayer passed in tears at the foot of the altar? It was God, preferred above all, loved more than all, with undivided heart, yet with no exclusions—for this love embraced, elevated, and intensified all legitimate affections. In the fire of charity, these affections became an ardent and consuming thirst for the salvation of souls.

Finally, as God offered Himself for us on the Cross, so the saints offered themselves to God, even to the point of martyrdom so that His will might be accomplished, that His Kingdom might be established in souls, and that He might be glorified. And when (as in the case of St. Dominic) they were unable to obtain martyrdom though ardently desiring it, they still experienced a daily death, though no less heroic, of labors, of pains and of continual tribulations. As God gave Himself to them as food, in the same way, they responded to His love and let themselves be consumed body and soul by Him, making themselves "food" of God.

St. Dominic, St. Catherine, St. Peter Martyr, St. Rose of Lima, St. Catherine of Ricci, St. Pius V, St. Louis Bertrand, and all the saints tell us the same thing through their lives, namely, that the ardent charity that burned in their hearts consumed them little by little, for this is the law of love. Love, which is as strong as death, makes us die to ourselves that we may be born to another life. There nothing is opposed any longer to the devouring flame because one is immersed in that fire of charity which is God. Such is the response of the saints to God's love.

Our Response

"Behold that heart which has so loved men that it spared nothing, even exhausting itself and consuming itself to attest its love to them. And yet from the greatest part of them I receive only ingratitude as shown by contempt, irreverence, sacrileges, and coldness that they have for Me and My Sacrament of Love. But what gives Me more pain is that it is a question of souls consecrated to Me" (St. Margaret Mary Alacoque).[1]

---

1 "And for this reason I am asking you that the first Friday after the octave of the most Holy Sacrament be dedicated to a particular feast to honor my Heart, making to it a reparation of love with honorable amends, receiving Holy Communion that day to repair the indignities that it has received when exposed on the altars. I promise you that my Heart will be enlarged to make

Of these four words, contempt, irreverence, sacrilege, and coldness, I fear that the last one is addressed to us. Coldness! The warmth of charity is not a sensible warmth. It is a wholly spiritual fire which continues to flame in the midst of the desolations and aridity with which God purifies our sensibility. But this love must be operative. It is certain that *all of us,* like all Christians, must respond with love to God's love because charity is a precept, not a counsel. Yet, is our love effective and operative or is it a self-satisfying, passive thing? Does it persist despite aridity and the desolations necessary to purify our sensibility? Are we disposed to go outside ourselves, to bend ourselves toward Our Lord, to humble ourselves as He humbled Himself? Are we dying to the sensible and natural life in order to live the life of Christ? Do we accept the daily sacrifice which the common life demands? Is our love like that of the saints?

The quality of our charity is not measured by the sweetness of a sensible devotion. The infallible signs of progress in charity are the hatred of sin and the configuration to Christ by means of progress in all the virtues and gifts of the Holy Spirit. If we do not wish to die to sin, if we do not wish to mortify ourselves, we do not love the Lord and we live the religious life in vain.

In religious communities, from what do disobedience, the harshness of judgment, the antipathies that are not overcome and the divisions derive? They are derived from not wishing to die to self. And yet we did not enter religious life except to die to self. In fact, only if we know how to die to ourselves will Christ be able to grow in us.

If this happens then not only the natural acquired virtues that the world can recognize will make themselves known in our life, but also those infinitely superior virtues which are the Christian virtues and gifts of the Holy Spirit. These include the

---

abundant graces descend upon those who tender it this honor and endeavor to have the feast accomplish its purpose."

spirit of faith which is nourished by thoughts of God; confident hope which relies exclusively on God; charity which unites us always more intimately to Him despite sadness, interior pains and tribulations of every kind and asks only the possibility of being poured out for one's neighbor; Christian prudence which is always much opposed to the prudence of the flesh; justice in dealing with our neighbor, which stops us from formulating even the smallest rash judgment about the soul of one of our confreres; fortitude which never draws back from the work fixed by God and patiently bears trials; and temperance which gradually makes the instinctive movements of our senses and of our heart docile, penetrating them with the divine life. Thus we shall also acquire, like the saints, a divine way of acting. The spirit of wisdom, understanding, knowledge, counsel, piety, fortitude, and fear will penetrate us more and more.

Then we shall not desire other than to give ourselves to God until death. Our love will find new nourishment in the daily labors and sacrifices of the common life. If our body is slowly consumed, we should remember that God is hungry for us. Just as He gave Himself to us as food, we ought to give ourselves to Him so that He may transform us into Himself and take us from this poor life here below, which is a death in comparison to the life that awaits us in Heaven.

CHAPTER V

Fraternal Charity

I have given them the glory You gave to Me, that they may be one as We are one—John 17:22

WHEN our soul is purified by mortification and renunciation, the supernatural light that is given us in prayer increases the love of God in us and permits us to accomplish, in a manner more and more perfect, the first precept of the Law: "You shall love the Lord, your God, with all your soul, with all your heart, with all your mind, with all your strength" (Mt. 22:37). But there is a second precept which derives necessarily from the first: "You must love your neighbor as yourself" (Mt. 22:39).

Love of neighbor is presented to us by Our Lord as a necessary consequence and sign of our love of God: "Just as I have loved you, you also must love one another. By this love you have for one another, everyone will know that you are My disciples" (Jn. 13:34–35). St. John has written: "Anyone who says, 'I love God', and hates his brother, is a liar" (1 Jn. 4:20).

One day Our Lord wanted to make Bl. Henry Suso, who had asked to be shown a truly perfect man, understand this truth. Bl. Henry had this vision. In the middle of a vast plain he saw a cross and at its foot a man of meek aspect and with a kind and gentle look; a little bit farther on there were two groups of men, very different among themselves, who were trying in vain to reach him. This man represented Christ and all those who have attained union with Christ, characterizing themselves by their mildness and gentleness. One of the two groups represented the intellectuals who contemplate and admire the truth, but do not put it into practice as perfection demands. The other group represented all those men who give themselves to all the practices taught by the authors on spirituality and to the greatest mortifications. Neither of the two groups could reach Christ, and for the same reason. Those who passed their life in contemplation, or rather in speculation, without putting these truths into practice, judged and condemned others without mercy; while those who made a profession of mortification condemned without mercy those who did not follow their way. These religious did not reach Christ because they did not love one another, and their lack of charity showed itself in the harshness of their judgment. Henry Suso gave thanks for this lesson and, though well advanced in perfection, beat his breast for having lacked fraternal charity and for having severely judged his confreres.

We ought to meditate on this great obligation of charity toward our neighbor. If we are lacking in it so many times or permit ourselves to develop an excessive affection other than that demanded of us by the Lord, it is because we do not understand in a practical way that fraternal charity is nothing other than the extension of the love that we ought to have for God. This love, essentially supernatural and theological, must extend to all our brothers. Therefore we should consider why the love of God ought to extend to our neighbor and how to practice fraternal charity.

Why the Love of God Ought to Extend Also to Our Neighbor

We must recognize that our nature leads us to love those who do us good, and to hate those who do us evil, while leaving us indifferent toward the others. Before the coming of Christ,

the Pharisees taught (Mt. 5:43): "You must love your neighbor";
but they added: "Hate your enemy." Our Lord says: "Love your
enemies and pray for those who persecute you; in this way you
will be sons of our Father in Heaven, for He causes His sun to
rise on bad men as well as good, and His rain to fall on honest
and dishonest men alike. For if you love those who love you,
what right have you to claim any credit? Even the tax collectors
do as much, do they not? And if you save your greetings for
your brothers, are you doing anything exceptional? Even the
pagans do as much, do they not? You must therefore be perfect
just as your Heavenly Father is perfect" (Mt. 5:44–48).

The fraternal charity demanded of us does not belong to the
natural order like the fraternity that can exist between pagans;
rather, it is essentially of the supernatural order. Natural love
makes us love our neighbor for the benefits that we have received
from him or for his good qualities. Charity, on the other hand,
makes us love our neighbor for God, because he is a son of God
or is called to become one.

Is it possible for us to love men with the same love with which
we love God? Even with the same divine love? The strictest
theology responds with a "yes," and explains this to us with a
very simple example. He who deeply loves a friend, also loves
the sons because he loves their father; and he loves the sons with
a true love which, in case of need, he also tries to demonstrate.

Therefore, if all men are sons of God or at least called to
become so, we ought to love them all, and love them in the
measure that we love our common Father. To love our neighbor
in a supernatural way it is sufficient to look at him with the eyes
of faith and to remember that, though he differs from us in
condition and character, he is still born, like us, not only of flesh,
of blood, and of the will of man, but of God (Jn. 1:13). Or, at
least, he is called to be born to the life of God, to participate
in the divine nature and eternal beatitude. Hence both of us

belong to the same family of God. How, then, can I not love him if I truly love God? But if I do not love him, yet pretend to love God, I certainly am lying (1 Jn. 4:20). If, on the other hand, I love him with this love, it is a sign that I love God since the love of God is the same love that is directed to the true supernatural reality of my neighbor. In other words, I love him because he is a son of God and a member of the Mystical Body of Christ, because the Holy Spirit dwells or wishes to dwell in him. I love him because he is destined to become, like me, a living stone of the Heavenly Jerusalem and, perhaps, a more precious and better worked stone. I love in him the realization of the divine idea that rules his destiny, and I can love him with a divine love because I love him for the glory that he will eternally give to God.

Sometimes the worldly will object: "But does this really mean loving man? Is this not rather loving only God and Christ in him? Man ought to be loved for himself." First of all, it might be mentioned that man as man cannot claim the right to a divine love. In reality, however, charity loves not only God in man but also man in God and for God because it loves what man ought to become, namely, an eternal part of the Mystical Body of Christ. Moreover, charity does all in its power so that man may be able to attain his true destiny. Also it loves what he already is through grace. If he does not have grace, charity loves his nature, not insofar as it is hostile to grace in consequence of original sin but insofar as it is capable of receiving grace. Charity loves man in himself, with the same love with which it loves God. Ultimately it loves him for God, for the glory he is called to give Him.

If this is so, it follows that we ought to love all men. All are, in fact, neighbors similar to ourselves, because all are created in the image of God and called to be part of His family and enjoy the same glory. Therefore, it is clear that we ought to love those also who are naturally indifferent to us, and even our enemies, because they do not cease, by this reason, from being sons of God or at least called to be such. Moreover, we ought to be disposed to help our enemies, at least if we should see them in a situation where they are reduced to a condition of extreme necessity and in urgent need of our help. This is a *precept*. When it is not a case of extreme need, Our Lord counsels us to help them.

Our charity should not know limits; it cannot exclude anyone on earth, in purgatory, or in Heaven. It stops only before hell. In fact, only the damned cannot be loved by charity because they no longer have the capacity of becoming sons of God, and, since they hate Him eternally and have neither the capacity nor the desire to be lifted up, they can no longer draw our compassion. Except for the unquestionable case of the damned, we ought to exercise our charity toward all, because charity knows no other limits than those of the very love in the heart of God.

We ought to love our neighbor as ourselves, that is, not for self-interest or pleasure, but desiring for him, as for ourselves, grace and glory which will be the glory of God. We should not, however, love him more than ourselves. We must prefer our own salvation to that of others. We cannot put ourselves at a distance from God to save our neighbor, although we may die for his salvation. Indeed, sometimes we have the obligation to do so, as when he is entrusted to us.

Charity, far from destroying natural love, raises it to the infinite, since it respects the natural order as it came from the hands of God. First of all, we ought to love God above every other thing, then our souls, then our neighbor, and lastly, our body. God wishes to reign in our heart, but He does not intend thereby to exclude all other affection that can be subordinated to that given to Him. On the contrary, He elevates it, making it grow daily in proportion to our progress in charity.

This fraternal charity should be like the love of God, not only affective but effective. It is enough to remember the example of the saints. St. Dominic sold his books to feed the poor and wished to sell himself as a slave to ransom a prisoner. The lives of the saints, like that of Our Lord, were a continual act of fraternal charity. Like their Master, they loved their brothers even to the Cross, even to martyrdom. They took the saying of the Lord literally: "Love one another as I have loved you" (Jn. 13:34). To announce the Gospel to their brothers they faced the worst sufferings.

How to Practice Fraternal Charity

The occasions that could tempt us to be lacking in fraternal charity are always present, even in a monastery or convent. The souls that one must live with are certainly chosen souls, but only to a certain point.

Whenever persons see each other from morning to night throughout the years, in the most varied states of mind and conditions—in sickness and in health, in pain and in joy—one cannot help but notice that together with his many virtues, his confrere also carries some true moral infirmities. A monastery is not yet Heaven; it is only the novitiate of Heaven, a school of perfection. Even if all the defects would disappear, the occasions for bruises and little conflicts would still exist because of the diversity of feeling, character, education, and because of the nervous tension that derives from such an intense life. They would exist also by reason of the fact that, while Our Lord seeks to unite, the Devil seeks to divide.

Providence intentionally permits the existence of many occasions so that we may humble ourselves and practice fraternal charity. "It is in weakness that virtue is made perfect" (2 Cor. 12:9). Our own miseries humble us, those of our neighbor make us practice virtue. Only in Heaven will the causes of discord completely disappear because there all the blessed will see in God, in His beatific light, what they should desire and do.

Here below, even the saints sometimes can be found disagreeing and inflexibly defending their own opposite points of view with the conviction that it is a question of the will of God. It so happened with St. Philip Neri and St. Charles Borromeo that they could not agree concerning the Oratorians of Milan. Thus, one had to recall his Oratorians to Rome, while the other instituted the Oblates of Mary at Milan.

In the midst of such difficulties as well as ever-recurring new ones, how can one practice fraternal charity? Two things are necessary: to look upon one's neighbor with the eyes of faith, that is, to discover in him the supernatural being that we ought to love; and to love him by bearing with him, making ourselves useful and asking God for the union of hearts.

First of all, we must look at our neighbor with the eyes of faith. Just as the love of God is born from faith in Him, so it is with charity toward our neighbor. It is necessary, therefore, to look at our neighbor with the gaze of faith in order to discover in him that supernatural reality which we ought to love. Since that which is divine in him is sometimes deeply hidden from our view—not by faults that are grave in the eyes of God, but by defects of temperament that irritate us and that subsist despite virtue—in order to see the divine in him, we must have a pure and attentive eye. We will see it, if we deserve to see it.

Just as the living water of prayer is not given except after the purification of renunciation, in the same way it is not granted us to see God in souls until we have become detached from ourselves. This is so, not only that we may see the beauty of a soul despite the differences of character, but also that we may simply be able to think to ourselves every time we come in contact with another: "This is a soul loved by God, in whom the Holy Spirit dwells; he or she is a member of the Mystical Body of Christ, called with me to the same beatitude, and, perhaps, to a level higher than mine."

This treats of a very simple thought, and yet, what Our Lord wants of us is found here. Jesus does not expect us to deceive ourselves in judging our neighbor. In fact, it is only supernatural benevolence that will enable us to see everything correctly. Rash judgment is, however, all too often set in opposition to this way of acting. The most frequent reproach that Our Lord directs towards us for lack of charity to our neighbor is concerned explicitly with rash judgment: "Do not judge" (Mt. 7:1). Rash judgment is essentially evil-minded. It is the decision of a judge who attributes to himself a jurisdiction that he does not have over the soul of his brothers. It is the verdict of a bribed judge, implacable, without mercy, who knows only how to condemn.

We see a slight indication of evil and immediately we affirm that evil exists in an evident way. We see two and affirm four. All this stems from egoism and pride. Let it be noted, further, that if it is a question of grave matter we commit a mortal sin.[1]

Our Lord is very severe in dealing with those who form rash judgments because they commit a double fault, against justice and against charity. They attribute to themselves a jurisdiction which they do not possess. In order to judge one should possess the testimony of a trial, but when it is a question of judging the interior intentions of our neighbor, we cannot have the testimony of a trial. In this case the only judge is God, who sees into the intimate part of the conscience, speaks to it, knows its ignorance, its errors, its difficulties, its temptations, its good will and its repentances.

Some persons pretend to know better than ourselves what we should say to God, and they set themselves up as our judges. "Without being aware of it," says St. Catherine of Siena, "we wish to dictate laws to the Holy Spirit and impose our way on

---

1 St. Thomas says, "If we cannot avoid the suspicion, we should at least refrain our judgments, that is, not formulate decisive and irrevocable judgments" (*S. T.* II II, Q. 60, a. 3). Cajetan and many others think that rash suspicion, when limited to doubt or opinion, is not in itself a mortal sin. Banez, Medina, Billuart are of the contrary opinion.

other souls; often our judgment is mistaken, and what is worse in the eyes of God, whatever may be the appearances of the benevolence that we seek to demonstrate, this judgment is evil-minded and comes from our egoism and pride." Instead of seeing our neighbor as a son of God, called to the same beatitude as ourselves, we see in him a rival, whom we want to overturn and abase.

We should pay attention and beat our breasts, because Our Lord said: "Do not judge, and you will not be judged; because the judgments you give are the judgments you will get" (Mt. 7:1–2). And how can we dare act like judges? Do we wish to take the speck from the eye of our brother, while we have a beam in our own? (cf. Mt. 7:3). And who can tell us that we might not fall this evening into a much graver offense than what we are condemning?

But, someone may say, if the evil is evident, does God then ask us to deceive ourselves? St. Catherine of Siena responds: "We must not see it to judge it and to murmur, but to have compassion and to assume its weight before God, according to the example of Our Lord." This is charity. If we restrain our rash judgment, we will accustom ourselves to seeing our neighbor with the eyes of faith, with a pure eye which is the very eye of God, and we will see in our neighbor the temple of the Holy Spirit, or, at least, the soul which He wants to approach and in which He wants to dwell.

It is not sufficient, however, to contemplate in the light of faith the supernatural being of our neighbor. We must also love him, bear with him, make ourselves useful, and desire a union of our hearts.

First of all it is necessary to *bear* the defects of our neighbor. What afflicts the saints to a great degree are the offenses made to God, while what afflicts us more and makes us lose our patience are external defects, which often are a small thing in the eyes of God. We endure some sinners without any difficulty, while certain virtuous persons make us exercise an enormous patience.

God wills that we bear with one another in charity. "Bear with one another charitably" (Eph. 4:2). He does not want us to be scandalized or irritated with the evil He permits. He does not want our zeal to be transformed into impatience or bitterness. And He does not want us to complain about others, coming to the point of being persuaded that the ideal is in us or at least that we love it while others do not. In short, He does not want us to pray the prayer of the Pharisee.

We should bear with one another without being scandalized by the evil that God permits in order to draw a greater good out of it. The art of God consists in drawing good from evil. It is precisely the scandal of evil that has made partially sterile so many attempted efforts to carry out reforms in the Church and in religious orders. We should support one another. Indeed, we should do something more. As St. Paul says, "You should carry each other's troubles" (Gal. 6:2), just as Our Lord carried the burdens of us all on His shoulders.

Perfection, however, does not consist only of bearing with one another but also in returning good for evil. Before all else we must give good example which edifies and we must *pray*. When we are tempted to judge our neighbor severely, to be scandalized or irritated, we should pray and light will shine in us and in the soul for whom we are praying. We will draw the blessings of God upon him. We should also pray for all the members of the community and for our superiors. Finally we should place ourselves at the *service* of all with humility and discretion. Then, with the aid of prayer, the union of hearts as well as the desire of Our Lord will be realized: "That they may be one as We are one" (Jn. 17:22).

In the first centuries this union characterized the life of the Church in the world. An intimate union existed between the Hebrew convert, the Greek, and the Roman; between the ignorant and the wise; between the rich and the poor. All formed one single family, that of the sons of God, and earthly goods were held in common. The disciples of Christ were truly recognized by the sign that He Himself had given them. The pagans were forced to exclaim: "Look how they love one another!"

With the propagation of the Church into the whole world, this profound union and intimate communion could no longer be maintained in the measure of earlier times. God wished, however, that such an example be preserved in the midst of men. This is one of the reasons for the institution of monasteries. Unity forms the truth, the goodness, and the beauty of a monastery. A disunited community is a living lie, according to the saying of St. John (1 Jn. 4:20): "Anyone who says, 'I love God', and hates his brother, is a liar."

In a monastery all is in common to manifest externally the union of hearts: the same dwelling, the same habit, the same rule, the same food, the same prayer in the same church, and, above all, the same Communion at the Sacred Table where all are nourished by the same body of Christ. But if the souls are not united, all is a lie before God, before men to whom they are proposed as an example, and also, before themselves. A disunited community is sterile, and it wounds the heart of God, who takes away His blessings.

If, on the other hand, with silence, abnegation, the spirit of faith, and charity, all the hearts are united, then all the souls are truly like the members of one same body. Each acts for all and all act for each. There is only one life, only one soul. It is no exaggeration to say "only one soul," because the Holy Spirit, Who vivifies all these souls, really inspires them and makes them act. Not in vain did Our Lord say: "That they may be one as We are one" (Jn. 17:22).

The Father and the Son are one through unity of nature, of thought, and of love. All Their activity has its termination in Their common and reciprocal love: in the Holy Spirit. So too in a fervent and united community, the souls ought to be entirely one through the unity of supernatural life, thought, and love. Their bond ought to be the same one that unites Father and Son, the common Spirit, that animates all of them.

O Soul of the Mystical Body, who vivifies the humanity of Christ, the head, and every one of His members, reveal to us the profound life and unity of this Body that is glorious in Heaven, suffers in purgatory, and struggles here below. Make us understand that even now we belong to the family of the saints and the family of God, and, despite the diversity of character, have us love one another as Christ loved us. Amen.

CHAPTER VI

Mortification

If anyone wants to be a follower of Mine, let him renounce himself and take up his cross and follow Me—Matthew 16:24

We always bear about in our body the mortification of Jesus, so that the life also of Jesus may be made manifest in our body—2 Corinthians 4:10; cf. Comm. of St. Thomas

WE have seen that our spiritual progress depends on our cooperation, which consists first of all in charity. Hence, we have the obligation of responding with love to God's love. We have already considered that this charity is not to be measured by the sensible satisfaction that sometimes accompanies devotion, but by two essential signs: death to sin and configuration to Christ through the increase of the Christian virtues. These are the two manifestations of progress in charity which we are to study now.

First of all Our Lord demands death to sin when He says: "If anyone wants to be a follower of Mine, let him renounce himself and take up his cross." "Let him renounce himself" is the law of mortification that we must impose on ourselves. "Let him carry his cross" is the obligation to bear patiently the trials Our Lord Himself imposes on us to purify us.

To make us understand that renunciation is not an end but rather a means that leads to light and an ever more ardent charity, the masters of the spiritual life have reserved the name "active purification" for mortification and that of "passive purification" for all the crosses that are sent us by God. Now I should like to talk to you in general about mortifications or "active purification." Afterwards we shall study it in greater detail, insisting on the spirit of the three vows of religion which regulate in a stable way mortification in our life.

In recent years, Naturalism, under the name of Modernism, attempted to depreciate mortification and in particular the religious vows, presenting them as a hindrance to the free development of the religious personality. They ask why we speak so much of mortification if Christianity is primarily a doctrine of life. Why speak so much of renunciation if Christianity is to engage the whole of human activity, instead of destroying it? Why speak so much of obedience if Christianity is a doctrine of liberty?

Why not appreciate our natural activity? Is it that our nature is not good? Was it not created by God? Our passions themselves as St. Thomas teaches, following Aristotle, are neither good nor bad. They are forces to be used. It is not necessary to mortify them but only moderate and regulate them. Why fight our own judgment and our will so much? This means falling into scruples and placing ourselves in such a state of slavery and dependence that we destroy all initiative, personality, and liberty within ourselves. It means belittling and degrading man under the pretext of divinizing him. Why condemn the life of the world since it is in this life that God has placed us and which we must lead?

The value of religious life is to be measured from its influence on social life. For it to exercise this influence it must not be hindered by an excessive preoccupation about renunciation, mortification, poverty, and obedience. On the contrary, we must allow free development to our spirit of initiative and all our natural aspirations. This will permit us to understand the men of our age and to come into contact with the world, which we must not so much combat as improve.

This preceding doctrine has been taught for some years in several religious circles. But, as always, the tree is judged by its fruit. We have seen that these innovating apostles, wishing excessively to please the world, instead of converting it allowed themselves to be converted by it; instead of assimilating souls to Christ, they let themselves be assimilated by the world, and little by little the salt became insipid.

We have all observed the consequences of this attitude. We have seen these apostles deny the effects of original sin and, something even more grave, slowly forget the infinite malice of sin as an offense against God. They have considered sin only insofar as it is an evil for man, a visible and palpable evil here below in society. Then they began to ignore the gravity of the sins of the spirit: unbelief, indocility toward the Holy See, presumption, and pride. In certain circles the gravest sin of all was considered to be abstention from social works, and, whatever might be its motive, it was always imputed to egoism. Meanwhile, true religion, and particularly the contemplative life, came to be considered as the destiny of all the unfit, of those incapable of any exterior activity. These apostles of a new kind, after having misunderstood the infinite gravity of sin, slowly came to forget the sublime loftiness of the supernatural end to which we are called. Instead of speaking to us about Heaven, about the vision of God, about configuration to the Word, they began to propose to us a vague moral ideal which, though colored by religion, seemed to disregard a future life and suppress the radical opposition between paradise and hell. Thus this new doctrine manifests its principle: Naturalism, the denial of the supernatural.

Necessity of Mortification

It is clear that these innovations have nothing in common with the doctrine of Our Lord and the Apostles, nor with the life of Christ and the saints. Our Lord did not come into this world for enjoyment and to perform a human work, but to do the will of His Father and realize the divine work of redemption which He accomplished by dying on the Cross. This was the aim of His whole life.

The saints have imitated Him. Let it suffice to recall the flagellations of St. Dominic; the mortifications of St. Catherine of Siena who, to conquer herself, forced herself to drink the blood of the wounds of the cancerous; what St. Antoninus did when he threw the key to his penitential shirt of iron into the Arno River so that he could no longer take it off. Remember St. Rose of Lima, Bl. Henry Suso, St. Louis Bertrand, and closer to us, Father Lacordaire. Did they give up the law of mortification?

Our Lord said: "If anyone wishes to follow Me, let him deny himself" (Lk. 9:23). And again: In order to sprout and reproduce, the grain of wheat must die (*cf.* Jn 12:24); He who refuses to die to himself and loves his soul in a manner that is too corporal, will lose it (*cf.* Jn 12:25); What does it benefit a man to gain the universe, the esteem of the world and fame, if he then loses his soul? (*cf.* Mt. 16:26).

St. Paul: original sin and its consequences. St. Paul does not only say that we must regulate and moderate our passions, but adds that we must punish our body to reduce it to servitude (1 Cor. 9:27). In our members is a law contrary to reason, that is, the flesh has desires in opposition to those of the spirit. He goes still further: "You cannot belong to Christ Jesus unless you crucify all self-indulgent passions and desires" (Gal. 5:24). The flesh or, as the Apostle says, "the old man" is not only the body. It is the whole man with his physical and moral life as born from Adam.

This natural man always remains in us here below, even after the grace of Christ has raised us up again, healed us, and has begun in us the work of deification, that is, of configuration to the Word. This natural man does not represent pure human nature as it came from the hands of God, but the erring nature oriented toward the earth, hungry for its own goods, desirous of its pleasures. It is man dominated by his immense unconscious egoism, dreaming of ultimate happiness here below. He is the so-called "go-getter" who desires only status. We find him represented everywhere, in all ranks, even among those who make profession of renunciation and humility.

This "old man" always lives in our nature devoid of grace. We must mortify him, reducing him in practice to impotence and sterility, not permitting him to bear his fruit, namely, sin. We live two lives, two contradictory lives, hostile and incompatible. One of the two must disappear that the other may develop.

It is true that our passions by their nature are neither good nor evil. They are forces to utilize, not destroy. Yet, after original sin our nature is inclined to evil, and it is this persistent inclination that we must definitely kill, mortify. In this Christian temperance differs from the purely natural temperance that the world knows. From this it can be deduced that if the dogma of original sin and its consequences forms an essential part of the doctrine of Christianity, then mortification is also an essential part.

Actual sin and its consequences. It is not only the consequences of original sin that impose mortification on us, but also actual sin and its consequences. Repeated actual sin generates vices. Although absolution, in restoring grace, gives us back the supernatural virtues opposed to these vices, these virtues are almost inoperative in us because their very unfolding and development remain so impeded by the bad dispositions that the vices leave behind, bad dispositions that remain in the temperament and often are almost unnoticed.

Not only must we moderate and regulate these consequences of sin but also destroy them since they constitute one of the most dangerous ferments that we carry within ourselves. Naturalism pays little attention to this because it ignores both the infinite gravity of sin as an offense against God and sin's profound consequences for the interior life of the soul in this life and the next. Since Naturalism is essentially superficial, it is content to establish a shallow harmony between spirit and body, between pride, egoism, and love of duty. It is not concerned with extirpating the remnants of sin which are a continual source of innumerable venial sins: sensuality, sloth, laxity, slander, calumny, rash judgments, pride, unbelief, presumption, and forgetfulness of God.

When venial sin is considered as something insignificant, when "it is drunk in like water," how can one be concerned with mortification or renunciation? If, on the other hand, sin is considered as the greatest of all evils, then mortification, which is basically none other than death to sin, must be an essential part of Christianity. Therefore, the true Christian understands that his first duty is that of doing penance, that is, detesting sin, feeling regret for it, avoiding it, and expiating it. This part of mortification is evidently necessary for all. Moreover, the Christian must practice humility, recognizing that alone, without the help of God, he can do nothing for his own salvation; that all he has from himself is infinitely inferior to what other souls have through grace. Hence, he must despise himself, that is, despise all in himself that is not from God but which is instead a deformation of the divine work.

Further, as the saints say and as St. Catherine of Siena continually repeated, the Christian must hate himself for love of divine justice. In other words, he must hate all in himself that is not from God and that injures the natural rights God has over his thought, his heart, his body, and his soul. He ought to be armed with a holy hatred for the remnants of sin that remain in him, and, as St. Paul says, crucify the flesh with its concupiscences.

Such are the rigorous laws against sin in the Gospel doctrine, unknown to the pagan world and the greatest philosophers. This asceticism, preached by John the Baptist even prior to Our Lord to prepare souls for His coming, is an essential part of Christianity.

Sublime Loftiness of the Supernatural End

There is, however, another reason for mortification that is also unknown to Naturalism. It is the sublime loftiness of the supernatural end to which Our Lord calls us. It compels us to detach ourselves from all that is earthly, all that makes us tend toward purely human works; it obliges us to fight against all the tendencies of the spirit and the heart that would absorb totally the soul's activity to the serious damage of the life of grace.

Our Lord imposed mortification on us the day on which in the Sermon on the Mount, He proclaimed the incomparable superiority of the New Law, the Law of Love, over the Old Law and that which was purely natural: "If your virtue goes no deeper than that of the Scribes and Pharisees, you will never get into the Kingdom of Heaven" (Mt. 5:20).

Mortification of all the feelings of anger, antipathy, and hatred. "You have learnt how it was said to our ancestors: 'You must not kill'. . .But I say this to you: anyone who is angry with his brother will answer for it before the court...So then, if you are bringing your offering to the altar and there remember that your brother has something against you, leave your offering there before the altar, go and be reconciled with your brother first. . ." (Mt. 5:21–24).

Mortification of the senses and of the heart. "You have learnt how it was said: 'You must not commit adultery.' But I say this to you: if a man looks at a woman lustfully, he has already committed

adultery with her in his heart. If your right eye should cause
you to sin, tear it out and throw it away; for it will do you less
harm to lose one part of you than to have your whole body
thrown into hell. And if your right hand should cause you to
sin, cut it off and throw it away; for it will do you less harm to
lose one part of you than to have your whole body go to hell"
(Mt. 5:27–30).

Our Lord next prohibits divorce, thus imposing *mortification in
Christian marriage*. When the partners cease to please one another
they are, nevertheless, obliged to remain united, a mortification
sometimes harsher than that of the cloister.

When it comes to the actual duties of charity, Jesus imposes
a *mortification of the heart, of one's judgment, and one's will* on a level
which the greatest philosophers never knew, and which many
Christians, even good ones, ignore. It transforms the practice
of the virtue of justice, absorbing it into charity. In our dealings
with our brothers we must think not only of their rights and
ours, but we must always be concerned with their soul, doing all
possible to make it better, yielding, always yielding so that their
soul may be illumined.

"You have learnt how it was said: 'Eye for eye and tooth for
tooth.' But I say this to you: offer the wicked man no resistance.
On the contrary, if anyone hits you on the right cheek, offer
him the other as well; if a man takes you to law and would have
your tunic, let him have your cloak as well. And if anyone orders
you to go one mile, go two miles with him. Give to anyone who
asks, and if anyone wants to borrow, do not turn away. You have
learnt how it was said: 'You must love your neighbor' and hate
your enemy. But I say this to you: love your enemies and pray for
those who persecute you; in this way you will be sons of your
Father in Heaven, for He causes His sun to rise on bad men as
well as good, and His rain to fall on honest and dishonest men
alike. For if you love those who love you, what right have you

to claim any credit? Even the tax collectors do as much, do they not?" (Mt. 5:38–46).

Why, then, this mortification of the senses, of the passions, of the heart? Why this mortification of one's will and judgment with the practice of Christian justice and charity? Because it is a question of being raised to a life infinitely higher than the natural life. You are not to be as the pagans. "You must therefore be perfect just as your Heavenly Father is perfect" (Mt. 5:48). Take care not to accomplish purely human works. You would receive here below only an exclusively human reward. Take care not to practice virtue to gain the esteem of men. You would receive your recompense here below but you would not have any in Heaven (*cf.* Mt. 6:1).

The life which we must attain is the life of the resurrected Christ, that is, a life which has passed through death. That life implies, not a superficial harmony, but that profound harmony between body and soul, between the soul and God, which was the privilege of the state of original justice and will be granted in the state of glory. We should be distrustful of a superficial harmony that is attained without any hard renunciation or mortification; it only seems real. Within us opposing principles struggle without our knowledge. An egoism and an unconscious pride are developed which, in certain circumstances, can be the source of very serious offenses, capable of dividing and killing the soul.

We should be most distrustful of that superficial harmony because, unless we acquire here below a profound harmony (supposing that we avoid mortal sin) we shall have to acquire it later, and through constraint, in purgatory. Those who do not want to experience mortification here below will be forced to experience it in the next life. These, then are the two principal motives for mortification: the consequences of sin and the elevation to a supernatural end. In other words, we must practice

mortification out of hatred for sin and for the love of God, our
ultimate end.

Ways of Mortification

Knowing why we should mortify ourselves is not enough. We
must also know how to mortify ourselves.

All the treatises on asceticism distinguish between exterior
and interior mortification. Both are necessary. In fact, the
mortification of the senses—of sight, hearing, taste, smell, and
touch, the doors through which temptation can penetrate—
would be of no help unless there were also mortifications of the
imagination and the memory. The imagination leads us to empty
fantasies with which the Devil can make a fool of us, and the
memory reminds us more often of the faults of our neighbor
than of his merits.

We must mortify our hearts. The Lord is not pleased with a
divided heart. He wants to reign in us. This certainly does not
exclude or forbid other affections; indeed, it's just the opposite.
But every affection must be subordinated to His love, if it is to
be truly supernatural and helpful for eternal salvation.

Furthermore, we must mortify our own judgment, often defiled
by prejudices and often a source of stubbornness, extravagant
ideas, and singularity of conduct. Above all, we have to mortify
our own will and egoism, which make us prisoners of our own
selves. This is the worst type of slavery, often unconscious and
therefore the more dangerous. It hampers any progress toward
God and renders our best actions defective. It is necessary to
make this egoism die because we are not the center and the
end of ourselves; we must conform our will so perfectly to the
divine will that they can never be separated.

Among all these tendencies that put us at a distance from the
love of God, it is important to discern the one which for us

constitutes the gravest danger, our predominant fault. Against this our efforts must be directed.

Let's suppose that we have done all possible to mortify our senses, our passions, and our heart, and that we have made a firm resolution to give ourselves completely to the interior life. But then, how many defects still exist in us and what a distance separates us from the religious ideal! To make ourselves aware of them, it would be necessary to read often the description St. John of the Cross gives of the defects of those who are beginning to dedicate themselves to the interior life. He finds in them the seven capital sins applied in a spiritual way, defects that can easily be reduced to two, spiritual sensuality and spiritual pride.

Spiritual sensuality, under which the Saint lists greed, lust, avarice, and spiritual sloth, consists of allowing oneself to be led astray by the sensible consolation poured into the soul at the beginning of the interior life. Many, misled by the attractiveness of consolations, seek these delightful affections rather than purity of heart and true devotion. They read all the books that treat this subject, spending more time on this than on performing meritorious acts. Under the pretext of a spiritual purpose, they have friendships with some people, much less for the glory of God than for the pleasure of talking about their feelings. They are never content with the gifts of God. And if the exercises of piety do not bring them consolations, they either abandon prayer out of laziness or, to regain what they have lost, they exhaust themselves by the weight of their penances, which they perform without discretion, without rule, and without obedience. Thus they have put themselves in a state of exhaustion in which they are prone to all sorts of temptations.

Is it necessary, then, to reject sensible devotion? Not at all! It is useful for our spiritual progress, especially in the beginning. Our Lord gives us the milk of consolation before nourishing us with the hard bread of tribulation. Yet, this sensible devotion is to be loved only as a means, not for itself but for God; and loved in the measure that it is useful for our eternal salvation. Therefore, we should not bewail excessively when Our Lord decides to deprive us of it.

Another defect of beginners (and how many among us always remain beginners!) is spiritual pride, a secret pride that comes from the fact that we reflect too much on our own fervor, being complacent in our selves and our actions, and easily induced to speak of spiritual things, making ourselves masters rather than disciples. We judge others and condemn them in our heart because they do not practice devotion in the same way we do. And so, in the end, we are acting like the Pharisee who became proud of his good works and despised the publican. "Often the Devil incites these beginners to fervor, and inspires in them the desire to undertake some good works in order to feed their presumption.

"This spiritual pride generates spiritual envy. The soul becomes saddened and is bothered by the good of those who surpass it in virtue. It can scarcely bear seeing them praised, and seeks to neutralize, as much as possible, the effect of the praises that are so liberally bestowed on them. The soul would like to be preferred to all.

"How contrary all this is to charity, which instead always takes joy in the spiritual good of those who are superior to us, inducing us to imitate them and not to be bothered by their superiority" (St. John of the Cross, *The Dark Night*, Book I, Chapter VII).

Here there is ample matter for mortification. We must be convinced that we shall have to fight to the end, because only in Heaven will all these seeds of sin die.

The spirit of mortification was taught by Our Lord when He said: "When you fast do not put on a gloomy look as the hypocrites do: they pull long faces to let men know they are fasting. I tell you solemnly, they have had their reward. But when you fast, put oil on your head and wash your face, so that no one will know you are fasting except your Father who sees all that is done in secret; and your Father who sees all that is done in secret will reward you" (Mt. 6:16–18). Our mortification should be joyous because it should be inspired primarily by the love of God. It is, in fact, for Him—to go toward Him—that we wish to destroy all seeds of sin in us. Every act of mortification, therefore, should be as a step of love toward God.

If we, then, elevate ourselves still more, love becomes adoration, and the manifestation of adoration owed to God is sacrifice, Christian mortification. What we contemplate in the saints is their sacrifice offered in union with the sacrifice of Our Lord on the Cross and on the altar. The flagellations of our own St. Dominic, for his sins and those of the faithful to whom he had to preach, were a sacrifice of expiation and also a propitiatory sacrifice to draw the grace of God upon souls. Above all, they were a sacrifice of adoration whereby the Saint reduced himself to nothing before God to acknowledge more fully that He is "He Who is" and that we, by ourselves, are nothing.

Effects of Mortification

Contrary to what Naturalism affirms, mortification leads to life—to the true life that comes to us from God and Christ and not from our fallen nature, our disordered passions, or from our pride. Christian mortification, far from debasing our personality, exalts it to such a point that it renders us independent of the world, its maxims, its theories, its fashions, its foolishness, and its snares. It exalts our soul above everything that is created, permitting us to depend only on ourselves and on God. In the measure that it makes our dependence on God closer, it develops our personality, rendering it more like the divine personality of

Christ. What personality is more marvelous than that of the saints? It goes beyond the limits of time and space, and after the passing of centuries it imposes itself on the admiration of the crowds without the help of any human means but solely through the superiority of wisdom and charity.

Mortification, then, does not constrain but liberates, because it alone sets us free from the slavery of our passions and public opinion, and, above all, from the slavery of egoism. This last is the worst type of slavery, the most difficult to destroy. More than any other it paralyzes our efforts toward the good. Mortification, furthermore, far from suffocating holy initiative and holy boldness, incites them since it teaches us not to rely upon ourselves but upon God. If there is a fruitful social endeavor, it is certainly that of the saints, always nourished by holy hatred of self. Who can even measure the social influence exerted by such a humble daughter of St. Dominic as was St. Catherine of Siena? Humility, abnegation, and renunciation hollowed out in her an abyss. Divine grace filled this up and she desired nothing other than to overflow on every side as an inexhaustible fountain of living water. Rivers of living water poured out from within her, because she was no longer Catherine of Siena. Her heart, her judgment, and her will had given way to the heart, judgment, and will of Christ.

Therefore, we should love mortification, meditate often on its motives—the consequences of sin in us and the sublime loftiness of the supernatural end to which Our Lord calls us. We should put it into practice without compromise, especially as regards our predominant fault. We should do this always with joy, with the interior joy of love, and always in the spirit of adoration. We should learn to immolate ourselves every day so that Our Lord may live in us and grant us to be other Christs who cause souls to be born to the divine life. May the Lord and the saints help us in this hard work which alone leads to true life!

CHAPTER VII

Humility

The Son of Man came not to be served but to serve, and to give His life as a ransom for many—Matthew 20:28

SINCE we are speaking primarily about the moral virtues that have a special affinity with the theological virtues and the life of union with God, it is necessary to reflect on what humility should be in those who wish to become proficient. The importance and nature of this Christian virtue demonstrate to us the gap that separates the acquired virtues described by pagan philosophers from the infused virtues of which the Gospel speaks.

Throughout the entire Christian tradition this virtue has been considered the foundation of the spiritual life. It is the foundation insofar as it separates us from pride which, according to Sacred Scripture, is the principle of all sin because it separates us from God. Often humility has been compared to the foundation that must be excavated in order to construct a building. The higher the desired building, the deeper the foundation has to be. The two outstanding columns of the temple to be raised are faith and hope, while charity is the dome.

Certainly humility should repress pride under all its forms, including intellectual and spiritual pride. Yet, the principal and most elevated act of humility is not precisely the actual repression of acts of pride. In fact, it is clear that in Our Lord and in the Blessed Virgin there was never a movement of pride to repress. There was in them, however, the uninterrupted, eminent practice of the virtue of humility. What, then, is the distinctive act of humility with respect to God and neighbor?

Humility with Respect to God

The distinctive act of humility consists in bowing down toward the ground (from the Latin *humus*[1] from which the name of this virtue is derived). To speak without employing a metaphor, this unique act consists in abasing oneself before God and before that which is of God in all creatures. To abase ourselves before the Most High means to recognize our inferiority, our smallness, and our indigence not only theoretically but also practically. Even in the state of innocence we would have been conscious of this, but after sin we become aware also of our state of misery.

Thus, humility is united to obedience and to religion. Yet, it differs from them. Obedience regards the authority of God and His precepts, while religion respects His excellence and the worship and adoration due Him. Humility, in making us bow down toward the ground, acknowledges our smallness and poverty, and in this way glorifies the grandeur of God. It sings His glory as did the Archangel St. Michael when he said: "Who is like God?"

The interior soul experiences a holy joy in reducing itself to nothing, so to speak, before God so that it may recognize in a practical way that He alone is great and that in comparison to His majesty all human grandeur is empty of truth, like a lie. Humility conceived in this manner is founded upon truth, especially on this truth, namely, that there is an infinite distance between the Creator and the creature. The more we realize this distance in a living and concrete way, the humbler we are. However elevated a creature may be, this chasm always remains infinite; and the more we elevate ourselves, the more evident this becomes.

---

1 Editor's note: *Humus* means soil, ground, earth.

Hence, the most elevated is the humblest because he is the most illumined. The Virgin Mary is the most humble of all the saints, while Our Lord is much humbler than His Mother.

The affinity of humility with the theological virtues can be seen by taking into consideration its twofold dogmatic foundation which was unknown to pagan philosophers. It is based, first of all, on the mystery of creation *ex nihilo*[2] which the philosophers of antiquity did not know, at least not explicitly, yet which reason can know with its natural powers. We were created from nothing. This is the foundation of humility according to the light of right reason. Under this aspect it is a question of acquired humility. Here we are concerned particularly with infused humility. Such humility is based on the mystery of grace, on the need for actual grace in order to perform the least act helpful for salvation. This mystery surpasses the natural powers of reason and is known only by faith. Our Lord expressed it in these words: "Cut off from Me you can do nothing" (Jn. 15:5)—in the order of salvation.

From this certain consequences flow relative to God, the Creator, His Providence, His goodness insofar as it is the source of grace, and His goodness insofar as it causes forgiveness of our sins.

First of all, regarding *God, the Creator,* we ought to acknowledge not only abstractly, but practically and concretely, that we by ourselves are nothing. "My substance is as nothing before You, O Lord!" (Ps. 39:6); "What do you have that was not given to you?" (1 Cor. 4:7). We were created from nothing by a *fiat*[3] of God, who is sovereignly free, and we are held in existence by His benevolent love, without which we would be annihilated in an instant. Although after creation there are diverse beings,

---

2   Editor's note: The Latin phrase *ex nihilo* means "out of nothing."

3   Editor's note: The Latin word *fiat* means "let it be done" or "let there be..."

nevertheless, reality, perfection, wisdom, and love are not increased because infinite wisdom and the fullness of divine perfection already existed even prior to creation. Besides, if all that comes from God were taken away from our most perfect free act, nothing, strictly speaking, would remain any longer, since this act is not produced in part by us and in part by God. Rather, the whole is from God insofar as He is its first cause, and the whole is ours insofar as we are the second cause. In the same way, the fruit of the tree is wholly from God as the first cause and wholly from the tree as the second cause. This must be acknowledged also in practice. Without God, Creator and Conserver of all things, we would be nonexistent.

In the same way, without God the supreme provider, without His *Providence* that "directs all things," our life would be totally lacking in direction. Consequently, we ought to receive with humility both the general direction of His precepts to attain eternal life, and the particular direction which the Most High has chosen from eternity for each of us. This particular direction is manifested to us by our superiors—the intermediaries between God and us, to whose counsels we should have recourse—and by events, as well as by the inspirations of the Holy Spirit. Therefore, we should humbly accept the position, perhaps very modest, that God has willed for each of us from all eternity.

Thus it is that in the religious life, according to the divine will, some ought to be like the branches of a tree, others like the blossoms, and still others like the roots hidden under the soil. Actually the roots, even if hidden, are more useful than the other parts since they draw from the soil the substance which makes the sap that is necessary for the nourishment of the tree. If all the roots were taken away the tree would die, while on the other hand it would not die if all the branches and blossoms were removed.

Humility, which induces the believer and the religious to accept willingly a hidden position, is very fruitful not only for themselves but also for others. In His life of sorrows, the Savior humbly sought the last place, permitted Barabbas to be preferred to Himself, and chose the scorn and shame of the Cross. Precisely for this reason in the building of the Kingdom of God Christ became the cornerstone. "Jesus said to them, 'Have you never read in the Scriptures: "It was the stone rejected by the builders that became the keystone. This was the Lord's doing and it is wonderful to see"?' " (Mt. 21:42). St. Paul writes to the Ephesians: "So you are no longer aliens or foreign visitors: you are citizens like all the saints, and part of God's household. You are part of a building that has the apostles and prophets for its foundations, and Christ Jesus Himself for its main cornerstone" (Eph. 2:19–20). Such is solid humility, marvelously fruitful, which even in the most hidden places sings the glory of God. It is necessary, therefore, to receive humbly from God the special direction that He has chosen for us, even though it has to lead us to a profound immolation. It is God who gives life and death (*cf.* Deut. 32:39. He leads us from one extreme to another. He humbles us and exalts us as He wishes (*cf.* 1 Kgs. 2:7). This is one of the most beautiful leitmotifs of the Bible.

Since we are unable to take the least step forward, or accomplish the least salvific or meritorious act without *the help of actual grace,* and we especially need it to persevere to the end, we should humbly ask for this grace.

Even if we possessed an elevated degree of sanctifying grace and charity, ten talents for example, we would still have need of actual grace for the least salvific act. Particularly we have need of the great gift of final perseverance for a happy death. We should humbly and confidently ask for this every day in the Hail Mary.

With St. Paul, Christian humility joyfully says: "Not that we are qualified in ourselves to claim anything as our own work: all our qualifications come from God" (2 Cor. 3:5) and "It is for that reason that I want you to understand that on the one hand no one can be speaking under the influence of the Holy Spirit and say, 'Curse Jesus,' and on the other hand, no one can say, 'Jesus is Lord' unless he is under the influence of the Holy Spirit" (1 Cor. 12:3).

In a word, humility ought to acknowledge in a practical way and more each day the grandeur of God, Creator and Provider of all things, the Author of grace. This humility, which recognizes our indigence, must be found in all the just. It must also be found in the innocent man.

After sin, however, we must acknowledge not only our indigence, but also our misery: the misery of our wretched and egoistic heart, of our inconstant will, of our irregular, violent, and capricious character; the misery of our spirit, which commits unpardonable forgetfulness and falls into contradictions that it can and ought to avoid; and the misery of pride and concupiscence, which leads to indifference concerning the glory of God and the salvation of souls.

This misery is less than nothingness itself since it constitutes a disorder, sometimes throwing our soul into a state of abjection that renders it worthy of contempt. The *Miserere* of the Divine Office often reminds us of these great truths:

> Have mercy on me, O God, according to Your great goodness; and according to the greatness of Your compassion, wipe out my offense.
> Thoroughly wash me from my guilt, and of my sin cleanse me.

For I acknowledge my offense, and my sin is before me always.

Indeed, in guilt was I born, and in sin my mother conceived me.

Cleanse me with hyssop, that I may be purified; wash me and I shall be whiter than snow.

Turn away Your face from my sins, and blot out all my guilt.

A clean heart give me, O God, and a steadfast spirit renew in me.

Give me back the joy of your salvation, and Your spirit of holiness take not from me (Ps. 51:3 ff.).

Yet who can detect his own failings? Absolve me from those that are hidden (Ps. 19:13).

How much different this abasement through true humility from that cowardliness born of human respect and spiritual sloth! Pusillanimity, contrary to magnanimity, flees from necessary work. Humility, far from being opposed to grandeur of soul, is intimately united to it. Thus the true Christian ought to aim at great things, worthy of a great heart. Yet, he should aim humbly and, if necessary, run the course of great humiliations. He must learn to say often: "Not to us, O Lord, not to us, but to Your Name give glory."

The pusillanimous is he who refuses to do what he can and ought to do. He can also sin mortally when he refuses to do what is obligatory. Humility, on the contrary, bows man before God, to put him in his true place. It does not abase us before God except to enable Him to act more freely in us. Far from being discouraged the humble soul places itself in the hands of God, and if by means of it the Lord does great things, it does not boast, just as the ax in the hands of the woodsman does not boast, nor the harp in the hands of the artist. It says with the

Holy Virgin: "Behold the handmaid of the Lord; be it done to me according to Your word" (Lk. 1:38)!

Humility with Respect to One's Neighbor

On this subject, St. Thomas, in a manner as simple as it is profound, says: "Each one ought to acknowledge that, in what he possesses through himself, he is inferior to all that every other person has received from God." Every man of himself has nothing other than his indigence, defectability, and deficiency. He ought to acknowledge, not only theoretically but also practically that all he has from himself is inferior to all that every other person has from God, both in the order of nature and that of grace.

The holy Doctor adds concisely: "The truly humble man considers himself inferior to others not because of external acts, but because he fears he may be accomplishing even the good he does through hidden pride." For this reason the Psalmist says: "Yet who can detect his own failings? Absolve me from those that are hidden." Or better, "Purify me, Lord, from my hidden faults." Moreover, St. Augustine says: "Believe that other persons, though in a hidden way, are better than you, although you seem to be morally superior to them."

Again with St. Augustine we must say: "There is not a sin committed by another which I could not commit because of my frailty; and if I have not committed it, it is because God in His mercy has not permitted it and has kept me in the good." Sacred Scripture says: "Lord, create in me a clean heart and a steadfast spirit; convert me to You, and I shall be converted; have mercy on me, a sinner, because I am weak and poor" (Ps. 51). St. Thomas writes: "Since the love of God for us is the cause of all good, no one would be better than another if he were not loved more by God" (*S. T.* q. 20, a. 3).

"What do you have that was not given to you?" (1 Cor. 4:7). This induces the saints to say to themselves on seeing a criminal condemned to death: "If this man had received the same graces that I have received for so many years, perhaps he would have been less unfaithful than I; and if God had permitted in my life the mistakes that He permitted in his, he would be in my place and I in his."

"What do you have that was not given to you?" This is the true foundation of Christian humility. All pride should be smashed under this divine saying! The humility of the saints thus becomes more and more profound, because they come to know better and better their own frailty in contrast to the grandeur and goodness of God. We must always aim toward this humility of the saints. But we should not employ the formulas that they used until we are profoundly convinced of their truth; otherwise, it would result in a false humility which would be, in comparison to the true, what rhinestones are in comparison to a diamond.

Humility toward one's neighbor, thus characterized by St. Thomas, differs immensely from human respect and pusillanimity. Human respect is the fear of the opinion and the anger of the wicked; this fear separates us from God. Cowardliness flees necessary work; it withdraws before great things that are to be accomplished and inclines toward pettiness. Humility bows us in a noble way before God and before what is divine in our neighbor.

The humble man does not give way to the power of the wicked, and in this he differs, says St. Thomas, from the ambitious man who abases himself more than required for attaining what he wants, and abases himself slavishly to attain power. Humility does not flee great things. On the contrary, it reinforces magnanimity, making the latter aim humbly toward elevated things. Humility and magnanimity are two complementary virtues that sustain one another like the two arches of a vault. These two virtues appeared splendidly in Our Lord when He said: "The Son of Man came not to be served but to serve [this is humility], and to give His life as a ransom for many [this is magnanimity with its zeal for the glory of God and the salvation of souls]" (Mt. 20:28).

It was not possible for Our Savior to aim at anything higher or to tend toward it with greater humility. He wished to give us eternal life, and to accomplish this He chose the way of humiliation, the Passion, and the Cross.

In due proportion, these same two apparently contradictory virtues are united in the saints. Thus, the humble John the Baptist did not fear the anger of Herod when he said to him: "What you are doing is not lawful" (cf. Mt. 14:4 and Mk. 6:18). The apostles in their humility have no fear of the opinion of men and are magnanimous even to martyrdom. There is something similar in all the saints. The more humble they are, the stronger they are and the less they fear human opinions however much they are to be feared. Such is the humble St. Vincent de Paul, fearless before the Jansenist pride, which he denounced in order to conserve for souls the grace of frequent Communion.

The Levels of Humility

Without humility it is impossible to have the perfection of charity. Then, what, practically speaking, do we have to do to attain the perfection of humility? Above all it is necessary to maintain the correct attitude with respect to praise and reproach.

Regarding praise, we must not commend ourselves. This would be to soil ourselves, as the proverb says: "He who acclaims himself, stains himself." Those who praise themselves find that they are never praised enough by others. We must not seek praises for we would make ourselves ridiculous and lose the merit of our good works. Finally, we must not be complacent with praises when we receive them. We could lose if not all the merit of our good actions, at least the flower of merit.

Concerning reproaches, we ought to accept patiently those we deserve, especially when superiors with the right and duty make them. If one becomes sulky, the benefit of this just correction is lost. Sometimes, it is also fitting to accept patiently a reproach that is hardly merited or totally undeserved. St. Thomas, when a novice, was unjustly corrected for an error in Latin while reading in the refectory. He corrected himself as he was told, but during recreation his surprised confreres asked him: "You were right, you read well; why did you correct yourself?" And St. Thomas replied: "Before God it is better to make an error in grammar than to be lacking in obedience and humility."

Finally, it is good to ask for the love of contempt, remembering the example of the saints. When Our Lord asked St. John of the Cross: "What do you want as a reward?" he answered: "To be despised and to suffer for your love." His prayer was heard. A few days later, in a very sorrowful episode, he was treated as an unworthy religious and in such a manner that is hard to imagine.

St. Francis of Assisi said to Brother Leo: "If, arriving late at night at the convent gate, the brother porter does not wish to open up for us, but takes us to be thieves and beats us with a stick leaving us all night in the rain and cold, it is then that we ought to say: 'What perfect joy! What joy, O Lord, to suffer for You and to become a little like You.' " The saints raised themselves to this point!

St. Anselm has excellently described the levels of humility:

(1) to acknowledge that under certain aspects we are worthy of contempt;
(2) to accept being so;
(3) to confess that we are so;
(4) to wish that our neighbor believe this;
(5) to bear it patiently when this is said of us;

(6) to accept, without reserve, being treated as a person worthy of contempt;

(7) to wish to be treated in this way.

These superior levels are described in all the books on piety, but, as St. Teresa says, "They are a gift of God; they are supernatural goods." They suppose a certain infused contemplation of the humility of Our Lord, who was crucified for us, and a living desire in us to become similar to Him.

It is certainly fitting to aim at this sublime perfection. Yet, few are the souls that attain it. Before attaining it the interior soul has many occasions to remember the words of Jesus, so simple and profound but truly imitable, at least in a relative way: "The Son of Man came not to be served but to serve, and to give His life as a ransom for many" (Mt. 20:28). This is the deepest humility, united to the noblest grandeur of soul.

One of the most beautiful formulas in which humility and magnanimity are reconciled is this one taken from the works of St. Thomas. "The servant of God ought always to consider himself a beginner and always to tend toward a more perfect and holier life, without ever stopping."

CHAPTER VIII

Poverty

Happy are the poor in spirit; theirs is the Kingdom of Heaven—Matthew 5:3

And everyone who has left houses, brothers, sisters, father, mother, children or land for the sake of My name will be repaid a hundred times, and also inherit eternal life—Matthew 19:29

WE have seen what mortification is in general. Now it is necessary to examine how it is organized in a permanent way in the religious state through the practice of the three vows.

The objections of Naturalism against Christian mortification naturally extend also to the religious vows. According to the naturalists, the vows are a hindrance, an impoverishment that condemns one to inactivity. This objection considers only the externals of the religious state, namely, that which has the prime purpose of protecting the heart of the state of consecration. Since its essence is wholly of the supernatural order, this escapes the notice of Naturalism.

The Religious State: State of Consecration that Presupposes Separation

If the religious life is considered only from the outside, it appears as a state of separation from the world, and it may indeed seem to be something very negative. Yet, if we observe it in its intimate being, or better, in its essence, we see that it is a state of consecration, of giving of self, and of belonging to God. Naturalism sees only the separation and cannot grasp the reason for it. It cannot see why this separation is required for the consecration which it safeguards. Consequently, it is very important to understand well the relationship existing between these two aspects, negative and positive, of the religious life.

Our Lord was consecrated and therefore separated. The religious state is the school of sanctity, the school of the imitation of Our Lord, who from His very birth was essentially and exclusively consecrated to God, consecrated in His nature itself. All His acts, even the most indifferent, proceeded from His divine personality and were referred to God through His love for His Father.

The soul of Our Lord is the domain where the Kingdom of God develops in all its fullness. Since Our Lord belongs exclusively to God, He cannot belong to the world. He was separated from the world, that is, separated from sin, from earthly goods, from honors, and daily worldly affairs (poverty); separated from pleasures, free from the needs of family life (chastity), so that even at the age of twelve He declared that He had to concern Himself with His Father's business; finally, He was separated from Himself, from His own will since He was not living for any other motive than to do the will of His Father, "to obey even to death, and to death on the Cross" (Phil. 2:9, obedience).

For us the contrary is true. Jesus, coming from above, is consecrated even from His birth. This transcendence separates Him. The religious, on the other hand, who makes profession of imitating Our Lord, comes from below, that is, from the world and from sin. Hence, he must first of all separate himself from the world that he may be able to consecrate himself to God and belong to Him alone.

Triple separation and triple consecration. For the religious soul to belong wholly to God, a triple separation and a triple consecration are necessary: separation and consecration of his external goods, separation and consecration of his body, and separation and consecration of his liberty. Only in this way will the harmony of the state of original justice be reestablished, insofar as this is possible here below. In the state of original justice there was a perfect harmony between the body and the external goods destined to serve the body, between the soul and the body destined to serve the soul, and finally, between God and the soul destined to serve God.

Original sin and sin in general disturb this triple harmony. Instead of making use of external goods, our body is led to make itself a slave of them, to accumulate riches. The miser becomes a slave of his treasure, the rich man a slave of his wealth and business, which absorb him entirely. Such is concupiscence of the eyes, never having enough of glitter and shine. After sin, the soul has the tendency to make itself a slave of the body, instead of using it. Such is the concupiscence of the flesh. Human liberty, carried to pride, refuses to be subject to God and to serve Him, thus becoming a slave of its own caprices. This is pride of life.

The purpose of the three vows is precisely to reestablish the original harmony. The vow of poverty separates us from external goods, consecrating them to God so that they may no longer be an obstacle, but rather a means. The vow of chastity separates us, so to speak, from our body, consecrating it to God so that it may no longer be an obstacle but a means for the life of the soul. The vow of obedience separates us from our will, from our liberty, consecrating it to God so that it may be fully subject to Him.

When we have abandoned to God our goods, our body, and our liberty, He transforms them so they can no longer be an occasion of disorder. He gives them back to us as the means to salvation. Fittingly we affirm of religious: "All belongs to you; but you belong to Christ, and Christ to God" (*cf.* 1 Cor. 3:22). This is the reason for the three vows of poverty, chastity, and obedience.

When these three virtues are subordinated to the virtue of religion, which has for its object the internal and external worship and adoration owed to God, the practice of poverty, chastity, and obedience becomes an act of religion. It is the oblation of ourselves to God, an oblation which, when total, merits the name of sacrifice and holocaust.

The religious soul, to make certain that it will not turn back but will persevere in the practice of these virtues, namely, poverty, chastity, obedience, and religion, binds itself to God with the three vows. These become a triple contract between God and us through which we obligate ourselves, for a certain time or even to death, to practice these virtues. Through such a contract, God obligates Himself, providing we are faithful, to give us what is necessary to lead us to sanctity. The vow is a means, a bulwark of virtue which extends much farther than the vow itself. Indeed, the virtue not only embraces what is obligatory in the religious life, but involves the sensitivity and generosity that constitute its perfection.

The vow, especially the perpetual vow, makes us become forever the property of God. It gives us, body and soul, to God. It gives to God our works, our prayer, our time, and our smallest actions. In return, God pledges to give Himself completely to us.

The Religious Value of Poverty

We will now consider religious poverty, the virtue of poverty that is essentially subordinated to the virtue of religion and which, under this aspect, merits the name of holy poverty. Religious poverty implies, as do all the religious virtues, a separation or renunciation together with a consecration.

Separation. Religious poverty implies essentially the renunciation of both property and of the free use of external goods for the love of God. If the motive of this renunciation or separation is not the love of God, one cannot speak of holy poverty, but at the most, of a philosophical poverty that disdains external goods through indifference, or in order to escape being bothered with them, or sometimes out of pride.

The renunciation demanded by holy poverty is not the privation of external goods. Hardship and misery are not holy poverty. We do not renounce external goods any more than we do our body or our liberty. We do renounce ownership and free use of these goods. Holy poverty forbids us to be attached to them with our heart. We should use these goods with a certain indifference, almost without being aware of them. We must always be ready to part with the objects we are using, including objects of piety. They remain only a means to our devotion whereas they could become obstacles if we become too attached to them.

Besides the actual ownership of goods, holy poverty forbids our free use of them. We should not use them, loan them, or give them away except with the explicit or, at least, the tacit permission of our superiors. We ought to limit ourselves to what is strictly necessary and avoid the superfluous. What is more comfortable becomes superfluous whenever what is less comfortable is sufficient. The best way of knowing what is necessary and what is not, is to conform ourselves to what is given to all—nothing more—unless there is a special reason, which, however, is always left to the judgment of the superior.

Holy poverty obliges us, moreover, to bear with patience and for the love of God, the accidental privation of something necessary when divine Providence permits this privation to test our patience and our trust. We should remember that rarely do we do, for the love of God, what very often is done in the world by the poor. They sometimes lack even bread to nourish themselves, clothing, heat, time to relax, doctors, and medicine for their health. We should acquire some strength to bear difficulties without complaining. If not, how could the practice of poverty be a mortification? How could it produce in us that religious strength and that joy, even in the midst of difficulties and privations, that Our Lord wishes to see in us so that we may be His image?

We ought to remember the extent to which Jesus was detached from the goods of this world. He was born in a stable and died on a cross. Nothing belonged to Him, not even the house He lived in at Nazareth. That belonged to His Mother, who died after Him. During His ministry He had nothing of His own, not even a place on which to rest His head. When they wished to proclaim Him king, He fled. The only glory that He sought was that of His Father. This glory, however, He sought, He wanted, and He demanded. We ought to be detached like Our Lord, like the saints, like our saintly Father Dominic who did not have even a personal cell or a bed on which to rest.

Consecration. Holy poverty does not involve only the renunciation of ownership and use of external goods. It assumes also the consecration of these goods to God. When we have turned them over to God, He concedes us the use of these goods on condition that we use them only for our salvation, for the salvation of souls, and for His greater glory. We can have beautiful convents, and especially beautiful churches, and still be practicing holy poverty. We possess these convents and churches for God, not for ourselves; they are not ours, but God's. Bl. Angelico was not lacking in poverty when he decorated the cells for the religious of Saint Mark's in Florence with frescoes that represented Our Lord's life.

In our monasteries we stand around Our Lord, not as beggars, but as sons. He gives us abundantly what is needed for soul and body. At the Sacred Table He gives Himself to us to nourish our souls. In the refectory He takes care that we have food to replenish the body. And what is "necessary" is not identical for all religious orders. The Lord distributes to each according to the nature and needs of its apostolate.

We can cease to be poor in two ways: by diverting these goods from their ultimate end, or by lacking trust in divine Providence. And these things we do to the extent that we make the goods of God serve our personal interests, outside any religious purpose. We also cease to be poor when we dissipate the goods of God, when we allow them to be damaged or lost, and when we waste time in dreaming or chatting—for our time belongs to God. The truly poor religious is hard working; and his work is that established by his rule, not anything else.

We are likewise wanting in holy poverty if, in moments when privation begins to make itself felt, we are lacking trust in divine Providence. In taking the vow of poverty, we signed an agreement with God and we have His signature. He has obligated Himself to provide us with what is necessary if we remain faithful to our duty, the specific purpose of our Order.

We should remember our father, St. Dominic. The brethren came to tell him: "Nothing more remains to eat." "Go to the refectory," said the man of God, and the angels descended from Heaven to serve the religious. It could not have been otherwise. Our Lord has given His word, and Dominic and his brethren had not been lacking in theirs. St. Agnes of Montepulciano, prioress at twenty years of age, found herself without any resources. Yet, she loved holy poverty, and knew how to surmount the difficulty despite the greatest privations. She had trust in the word of God. The Lord left her temporarily without anything only to test her love.

Why then should we be anxious? The Lord said to all Christians: "That is why I am telling you not to worry about your life and what you are to eat, nor about your body and how you are to clothe it. Surely life means more than food, and the body more than clothing! Look at the birds in the sky. They do not sow or reap or gather into barns; yet your Heavenly Father feeds them. Are you not worth much more than they are?. . .So do not worry; do not say, 'What are we to eat? What are we to drink? How are we to be clothed?' It is the pagans who set their hearts on all these things. Your Heavenly Father knows you need them all. Set your hearts on His Kingdom first, and on His righteousness, and all these other things will be given you as well" (Mt. 6:25–33). If Jesus has made this infallible promise to all Christians, what will He not do for His religious who have placed their lives in His hands?

St. Teresa has written: "The less we have, the less anxious I am. Our Lord knows very well that I experience more displeasure when the alms go beyond what is necessary than when something is lacking. And still I cannot say that we have been in need, such is the readiness of our adorable Master to come and help us" (*The Way of Perfection,* chap. 2).

We should strive to have this marvelous supernatural and divine trust. In moments of necessity we should never omit the prayers Our Lord demands that we perform, in order to do material works that He does not want. We should never transform the monastery into a workshop to procure our necessities nor should we seek to attract alms solely by human means.

We should strive to be faithful to the Lord in the observance of our rule and He, likewise, will be faithful to us. Just as God gave His word to St. Dominic, St. Agnes, and St. Teresa, so He has also given His word to us. Our Lord has said: "Happy are the poor in spirit; theirs is the Kingdom of Heaven" (Mt. 5:3) He does not say "will be," but "is."

Such is holy poverty under its two aspects, negative and positive, of separation and consecration. External goods are no longer an obstacle since they no longer absorb us, no longer preoccupy us. We use them to maintain the life of our body, for the salvation of souls, and for the glory of God.

Thus, in a monastery, by means of holy poverty, material goods themselves render worship and adoration to God, the ultimate end of all creation. Original harmony is reestablished. Freeing us from a thousand temporal concerns, holy poverty permits us to think about God and souls, to run along the road of perfection, and to live only for God and souls. Who can say what the fruitfulness of holy poverty will be under this aspect? It is enough to visit some convents dedicated to the help of the poor and the sick, or to teaching.

Still there is another fruitfulness that is purely spiritual. Holy poverty teaches us to practice many virtues, such as patience, humility, meekness. Above all, if we are docile, it communicates to us the spirit of detachment in such fullness that we are motivated to practice it not only in regard to material goods, but also in regard to the spiritual goods of intellect, heart, and soul.

The goods of intelligence are the various forms of knowledge; the goods of the heart are the affections; and the goods of the soul are spiritual consolations and our merits. Holy poverty teaches us not to consider as our own property the knowledge and small capacities we may have, because all this belongs to God. We ought to be detached from them; otherwise, this private possession that we have usurped will make us fall into pride.

We ought to consecrate to God our intellectual work, that is, to study what God wills, when He wills, as He wills, solely for His service, for His worship and adoration, for His glory.

The life of the saints tells us clearly enough how pleased Our Lord is to pour His light on souls detached from their own personal ideas. We might recall, for example, how much the insights of a St. Catherine of Siena surpass the highest theological contemplation.

Holy poverty teaches us to be detached from our affections. If, on the contrary, we wish to remain attached to them, they will bring about a great waste of time that we owe to God and to souls. These affections will be for us a danger of falling into sentimentalism or into still graver faults. We must consecrate our affections to God and place them under the supernatural influence of the virtues of charity and religion. Then they will grow and Our Lord will reveal to us all the treasures of a friendship that is truly supernatural. Holy poverty also teaches us to be content when we are not loved by some confreres or superiors. Is not the love of Jesus sufficient?

Poverty of spirit detaches us from the goods of the soul, that is, from spiritual consolations. It teaches us not to seek them for themselves as an end—a very dangerous thing—since in so doing we offer a weapon to the Devil. They ought to be desired only for God, as a means. One ought to accept being deprived of them when the Lord deems it necessary.

Poverty of spirit teaches us not to envy the graces given to other souls, and not to wish to become saints immediately without passing through the grades of intermediate trials. It teaches us to thank God when He takes from us the esteem of men and keeps us in humility by leaving us in our miseries. Further, it teaches us to despoil ourselves of our merits and to offer them to Our Lord and to the Holy Virgin for the salvation of needy souls. In this case, by despoiling ourselves we shall receive more than we give; indeed, we shall receive the hundredfold.

Finally, this voluntary *kenosis* prepares us for what God wishes to perform in us to ready us for the life in Heaven; to prepare us for that emptying of all that is human in us, for that interior crucifixion, for that nakedness of soul which for the saints begins and ends here below, while for the others it is accomplished in purgatory.

May the Lord grant that we dispose our soul to the work of a wholly divine purification which He alone can accomplish in us!

CHAPTER IX

Chastity

Happy the pure in heart: they shall see God—Matthew 5:8

WE have considered how holy poverty consists of the renunciation of external goods and in the consecration of these goods to the service of God. Religious chastity involves these two elements also: supernatural detachment from the pleasures of the body and the consecration of our body to God so that it may be a faithful servant in the work of our salvation, of the salvation of souls, and of the glory of God.

As for this separation and this consecration we ought to meditate particularly on the following aspects:

(1) The aim of this renunciation is to flee the servitude of the senses in order to be united to God, a thing that would not be necessary in the state of innocence.

(2) This renunciation consists in giving up ownership and free use of one's body.

(3) The principle of this renunciation is the grace deriving from mortification.

Separation

(1) The aim of this renunciation of matrimony and the pleasures of the senses is to flee the enslavement of the senses in order to unite ourselves to God. The unbeliever cannot understand this renunciation since he sees it as a negative perfection

and unnatural. He holds the qualities of the mother of a family much superior to those of a woman religious. In reality, this renunciation became a perfection only in consequence of original sin. It had no reason for existence in the state of innocence (*S.T.* I, q. 98, a. 2 ad 3), because in that state the body was perfectly subject to the soul, the passions perfectly docile to right reason, and the pleasures of the senses did not have that immoderate ardor that throws the soul into uneasiness and agitation and weighs it down, thus diverting it from contemplation of divine things.

Only as a consequence of original sin is virginity to be preferred to matrimony (*S.T.* II-II, q. 152, a. 4; and definition of the Council of Trent, sess. 24, can. 10 against Calvin and Luther). The observance of absolute chastity in the religious life tends precisely, by means of the privation of the pleasures of the senses, to reestablish the original harmony of soul and body, and to render the body so docile that the soul no longer experiences any agitation and can fully live its spiritual life.

"This absolute chastity," says St. Thomas, "cannot be practiced by all; but if it is necessary that some embrace the marriage state to assure the corporeal conservation of the human race, it is fitting that others abstain from it to devote themselves to the contemplation of divine things and thus contribute to the beauty and salvation of the whole human race" (*cf. S.T.* II-II, q. 152, a. 2 ad 1). The renunciation that religious chastity demands is, therefore, essentially related to our state of fallen nature. It is because the furnace of concupiscence remains in us after sin that God invites us to chastity.

Furthermore, the motive of this renunciation is the love of God. Detachment from the pleasures of the body through insensibility or through philosophic disdain does not constitute holy chastity. Some philosophers have abstained from the pleasures of the flesh to devote themselves to study (as St.

Catherine of Siena notes) but we, instead, ought to do this for love of God.

(2) Of what does this renunciation consist? It is not in separating ourselves from our body, but in giving up its ownership and its free use. By religious profession our body belongs to God; it becomes His. The profanation of this body, then, would be a sacrilege, just as in marriage the body of one spouse belongs to the other and its profanation would be adultery. We may no longer make free use of our body. We ought even to renounce every affection of our heart that is extraneous to the love of God. This is something indispensable.

(3) How are we to attain this renunciation? It is a gift of God, a supernatural infused virtue. Yet, God does not preserve it in us without our help. He wishes our cooperation, and calls for a twofold mortification, that of the flesh and that of the heart.

Without the mortification of the flesh it is impossible to practice holy chastity. For this reason our Constitutions prescribe fasting, abstinence, and vigils. We should not deprive ourselves of these obligatory helps. It is the least we can do.

But the mortification of the flesh is absolutely insufficient without mortification of the heart. In this regard the saints have given us the most beneficial warnings. Bl. Angela of Foligno writes: "Every affection of the heart is dangerous, even that which we have for God, if it is not what it should be. Love is the center where all good is contained and the center where all evil is contained. Nothing on earth, neither creature nor dominion, is so terrible as love, because no power penetrates the soul, the mind, the heart as it does. If this force is not regulated, the soul rushes frivolously into all snares, and its love is its ruin. I am not speaking only of a love that is absolutely sinful, where the danger of going to hell escapes no one. I am also speaking of the love of God and neighbor when it is not what it ought to be. When the love of God is not accompanied by discernment and mortification of the heart, it leads to death and to illusion. Whoever loves God in order to be preserved from some accidental suffering or to taste some spiritual sweetness, does not love in the right order. He loves himself first, and then God" (chap. 64).

He thus abuses what is most holy—God and His gifts—and he offers support to all the temptations of the Devil. The spiritual joys that he seeks for themselves stir up the passions sleeping in his heart of flesh. In this way, instead of taking the road that leads to the summits, where St. Catherine of Siena and St. Teresa lived, he slides inevitably down the descent, where Madame Guyon and other false mystics who ended up even more miserably let themselves be dragged. The worst corruption is that of the well-endowed soul. (The corruption of the best is the worst!) There is nothing more elevated than true mysticism, nothing worse than the false.

The spiritual love of one's neighbor or one's friend is also extremely dangerous unless it is accompanied by a profound discretion and mortification of the heart. Otherwise, it becomes useless, harmful, and carnal. The soul that has made the vow of chastity has become the property of God. It ought, therefore, to reserve for Him this heart that no longer belongs to self, and forbid all affection extraneous to charity. Instead, it sometimes wastes the time owed to God in useless conversations and dangerous dreams. If the person loved is wounded with the same arrow, the danger increases. "The hearts are attached, one to the other, and wisdom is not in them," says Bl. Angela of Foligno.

The day will come when these souls will be left blinded and will no longer see any evil in the most dangerous of liberties. They are sliding, and sometimes it is only at the bottom of the abyss, after the offense, that they wake up and open their eyes.

St. Teresa, in a celebrated chapter (chap. 4) of her *Way of Perfection,* says that certain particular friendships are a true plague that, little by little, kills fervor and destroys normal life. Such a plague generates profound divisions in the common life and compromises salvation. Many vocations are lost in the novitiate, or sometimes later, through an attachment that is too natural and too sensible, which, becoming stronger and stronger, separates one more and more from God.

Is all spiritual friendship, then, to be condemned? Not at all! It would be like condemning in totality the whole mystical life, with the pretext that there is a false mysticism. Spiritual friendship and true mysticism are those accompanied by discretion and mortification of the heart. Some friendships are truly a grace and a help that comes from God. Models of such friendships are that of St. Catherine of Siena and Bl. Raymond of Capua, a profound and supernatural friendship, full of self-denial, as is evident to us from the splendid letters that have been preserved; and that of St. Teresa and St. John of the Cross. "When reciprocal love is directed to serving the Lord, it can be recognized by the effects. In such a friendship there is no passion, and nothing other is sought than to encourage each other to conquer further passions. I would like to see many of these friendships between religious in large monasteries. But for this small house (of Avila) where we are, and in which we can be only thirteen, all the religious ought to be friends; all ought to love one another with warmth and to help each other" (St. Teresa, *Way of Perfection,* chap. 4).

These friendships, highly exalted and highly useful, are the fruit of mortification of the heart, which is their true guardian, and which, preventing them from deviating, permits them to grow until they become blended with charity. "Only those who have acquired the knowledge and the power of separating themselves immediately from anything, when they want to, can come together without fear" (Angela of Foligno, chap. 64).

Such is the renunciation and the twofold mortification of the flesh and heart that holy chastity imposes on us. Thus, it is especially a separation.

Consecration

As we have said, holy chastity is also a consecration of our body and heart to God. The effect of this consecration is:

(1) to make the body more similar to the soul;
(2) to make the soul more and more similar to God;
(3) to unite the soul to God with the bonds of a true marriage, in comparison to which the marriage of earth is only a symbol and shadow.

(1) First of all, a body living only for the soul becomes more similar to it, just as a friend takes on, little by little, the habits and tastes of his friend. What is the soul? It is a spiritual substance which we have never seen. Allow me to cite what one of the better preachers of our Order writes on this subject. "To see a soul it would be necessary to have the purely intellectual sight of the angels. We do know, however, that it must be absolutely simple, of a radiant beauty much superior to all sensible beauties, and serene and incorruptible."

The soul must be *simple* because it is not composed of extended parts like the body. It must be *beautiful* because it is pure, without admixture of matter; beautiful like beautiful doctrines, beautiful ideas, and beautiful actions, because the soul's intellectual and sensible faculties are its adequate and harmonious expression. The soul must be *serene* because it is immaterial, and therefore not disquieted by that which, being made of matter, is subject to movement, agitation, turbulence. Finally, it must be *incorruptible,* because it is simple. What is lacking in parts cannot be decomposed or corrupted.

Even the body through purity becomes in its own way simple, beautiful, calm, and incorruptible: simple as the veil of a virgin, simple as the attitude of a small child. Only two beings, by reason of their purity, are simple, the baby and the saint. The former is because he does not know evil; the latter because he has forgotten it by the effort of overcoming it.

The body, by means of purity, becomes beautiful because all that is pure is beautiful. The sky is beautiful when it is clear; the diamond is beautiful because it is pure, allowing itself to be penetrated by light; the human body is beautiful when it is pure, allowing itself to be penetrated by the soul whose reflection and expression it becomes. What makes the faces reproduced by Bl. Angelico so beautiful, if not their purity wherein the whole soul is transparent? Vice, on the other hand, disfigures.

With purity the body becomes calm. When purity is lost, noise and all that is showy and clamorous are sought. When one is converted, calm, solitude and recollection are sought. The attitude of a virgin is calm; that of the worldly person is noisy and agitated.

Finally, with purity the body becomes in its own way incorruptible. Purity preserves the body, while vice withers it, destroying and killing it. In the state of innocence, the body would have had the privilege of incorruptibility which the soul has by its nature. Still, purity leaves behind itself a trace of this original privilege. The body of some saints after death often remains incorrupt and gives off a delightful fragrance.

The purest bodies—those of Our Lord and of the Blessed Virgin—did not have to know the corruption of the grave. The body of our holy father Dominic was found intact and it gave off a most pleasing fragrance when his grave was opened. The body of St. Catherine of Alexandria, the philosopher, was carried by angels to Mount Sinai after her martyrdom.

(2) Chastity produces in the soul another superior effect. It makes the soul similar to God and unites it to Him with the bond of a true marriage.

We first note that the principal attributes of God are: power, which belongs more particularly to the Father; light, which belongs in a special way to the Son, the Word of God and Splendor of the Father; and love, which belongs more particularly to the Holy Spirit, the expression of the common love of the Father and the Son. We can see that with holy chastity the soul becomes powerful, strong, and luminous, participating in the divine Love in a manner so intimate that it truly becomes the bride of the Incarnate Word, the beloved daughter of the Father of Our Lord Jesus Christ.

With chastity the soul becomes powerful and strong. Suffice it to recall the courage of the Christian virgins who desired martyrdom, as did St. Cecilia, St. Agnes, St. Catherine, St. Lucy. They displayed a courage so superhuman that it terrified their executioners—an obvious miracle, and show of God's power. By means of chastity the soul becomes luminous: "Happy the pure in heart; they shall see God." The great seers—St. John, St. Paul, St. Thomas Aquinas—were virgins. St. Thomas Aquinas, freed forever at eighteen from the temptations of the flesh, consecrated his whole life to the contemplation of divine truths.

Often what theologians have not seen has been anticipated and intuited by Christian virgins, such as St. Catherine of Siena and St. Therese of Jesus, through the clearsightedness of their love. Frequently the theologian stops at the truth of God. The apostle goes beyond the truth to delight in the divine goodness also. Meanwhile, the contemplative virgin goes beyond the truth and the goodness to the beauty of God itself which is as the brightness and splendor of all His perfections taken together.

Of what value is the purely sensible beauty of even the most harmonious features in comparison with the spiritual beauty of a sublime doctrine or a heroic life? What is there here below more beautiful than the life of a saint? And yet the beauty of a saint is still partial and limited. St. Dominic excels for his love of God and neighbor, St. Thomas for his wisdom, St. Antoninus for his prudence, St. Peter Martyr for his faith, St. Vincent Ferrer for his love of divine justice, and St. Louis Bertrand for his gift of fear of God.

What a marvel to be able to contemplate the supreme harmony of all the divine attributes, the sublime accord between the most inexorable justice and the most tender mercy realized in that eminent quality of love so sublime that it is the source of these qualities which, in appearance, seem very contradictory! Here below we see contrasts. Chastity, however, makes the soul so luminous that it can intuit the most exalted harmony. Consequently, it is not surprising that the most outstanding words on how justice and mercy are to be reconciled were written by a soul that had rehabilitated itself through heroic chastity in the midst of the most terrible temptations, Bl. Angela of Foligno, who writes: "Nothing destroys harmony for me. I see the goodness of God in one saint and in all the saints, just as in one damned soul and in all the damned" (chap. 24). Heaven shows forth the diffusion of God's goodness and love; hell expresses His sacrosanct rights. Yet, it is always His goodness that is given and affirmed.

(3) Finally, the Christian virgin understands all the beauty of Jesus, and follows Him in all the acts of His life, from the manger to the Cross, as well as in His present-day work in souls. "In what splendor He has manifested Himself to the eyes of the

heart that see wisdom! Jesus did not reign, nor amaze the world with His discoveries. That is not His way of sanctity. On the contrary, He was humble and holy, holy before God, terrible in front of the Devil, without stain of sin!" (Pascal).

The Christian virgin, more than any other person, knows the secrets which unite on the Cross the most heroic strength and the tenderest passion, the most profound anguish and the most sublime serenity, the overflowing of sorrow and the most perfect happiness. All these beauties charm the Bride of the Canticle of Canticles. This spectacle of the Cross gives birth to a love stronger than death.

It is really holy chastity that enables the consecrated soul to love the Lord with the love of a bride. The soul is thus united to Him with the bonds of a marriage. Earthly marriage is only a symbol and shadow in comparison to these bonds, for the true realities are those of the life of the spirit.

The value of earthly marriage derives from a union that is holy, strong, sweet and at the same time fruitful. Notice how all these perfections are magnified to the infinite in spiritual marriage! If earthly marriage is *holy* it is because, as St. Paul says, it is the image of the intimate and mysterious union that exists between Our Lord and His Church (*cf.* Eph. 5:23). It cannot be its image unless it implies, not only the union of bodies, but also that of the souls of the two spouses. The spiritual marriage between Our Lord and the soul consecrated to Him is holy in itself because it unites us to the fountain of all sanctity, and helps give the Church its character of holiness. By this, the Church is distinguished from all other societies.

If earthly marriage is *strong,* it is because it is an indissoluble and reciprocal contract that supposes rights, duties and reciprocal services. Spiritual marriage is also indissoluble through rights—not only until death, but for eternity—and it implies such a reciprocity of rights that the consecrated soul can say to the Lord: "My beloved is mine and I am his" (Cant. 2:16). A little creature can speak of an infinite God as if the Almighty belonged to it alone. It has a right to God's love, one can say almost to His services, for God has given it His heart and it has become His collaborator. The religious nun is the collaborator of the Lord in establishing His Kingdom in souls. By her life she demonstrates in a practical way the truth of the doctrine of Jesus. She preaches by her example and with an eloquence in a way that words cannot equal.

If earthly marriage is a very *sweet* union, it is because of the intimacy that is assumed with the revelation of the most secret thoughts, and by the perfect communion of ideas, feelings, and wishes. But see how much this intimacy is surpassed by the union between Our Lord and His brides! Our Lord hides nothing from the faithful soul. "There are a thousand things that it knows, sees, senses, feels and is able to do—things that it alone is able to see, know, sense, feel, and be capable of."

The Eucharist truly reveals itself as the daily testimony of this love and union of bodies and souls. "The holy soul shares with Our Lord all His sentiments, suffers with Him all His pains, shares His joys, participates in all His ambitions, His jealousies, and, if necessary, His angers." Like Magdalen, it washes His feet and anoints them with perfume. The will is fully one with that of Christ. It has a burning zeal for the salvation of souls and thoroughly understands all the force of these words of the Bridegroom: "I have come to bring fire to the earth, and how I wish it were blazing already!" (Lk. 12:49).

Finally, the *fruitfulness* of earthly marriage procures for God faithful servants and sons. But the bride of Our Lord, freed through holy chastity from all the exigencies of family life, becomes also a *mother* in the plan of the propagation of souls. This soul gives itself to the poor, the sick, and the needy souls whom it raises to the supernatural life by its mortification, prayers, abnegation, counsels, and exhortations. To convert sinners, preserve the just, fashion the saints, it is for this that the soul labors without rest, instructing the spirit and assisting the body.

Is it not to this faithful bride, above all, to this mother who gives herself totally that Our Lord will say: "I was thirsty and you gave Me to drink; I was hungry and you gave Me to eat; I was naked and you covered Me; sick and you visited Me; in prison and you came to Me. Amen, amen, I say to you, he who renders these services to the least of My brethren, renders them to Me"?

This is the spiritual maternity which we all achieve if we are simply faithful to the grace of our state. Is this not the hundredfold, even here below, promised by Our Lord to those who leave all to follow Him?

Sons and daughters of St. Dominic, we ought to love this sublime virtue in a special way. It is a privilege of Christianity, as Father Lacordaire says, and, we can add, an "honor of our Order," which has been called by the Supreme Pontiffs, *Ordo Lilium*, the Order of Lilies. St. Dominic, so pure and so luminous, who carries a lily in his hand and a star on his forehead, at the hour of his death left us this last exhortation: "Let us be pure, and we shall pass through the world illuminating it."

CHAPTER X

Obedience

> *Be obedient to the men who are called*
> *your masters in this world. . .as you are*
> *obedient to Christ*—Ephesians 6:5; cf.
> *Hebrews 13:28*
>
> *The speech of the obedient will always be*
> *heard*—Proverbs 21:28
>
> *Explain to me how to keep your precepts,*
> *that I may meditate on your marvels*—
> *Psalm 119:27*

AFTER having considered how the harmony between the body and external goods is reestablished here below by means of holy poverty, and how the harmony between soul and body is reestablished by holy chastity, it remains for us to see how holy obedience reestablishes the harmony between our soul and God, which was disturbed by sin.

This third disorder, which is called by Sacred Scripture "the pride of life," is the love of absolute independence, the refusal to acknowledge an authority superior to ourselves. It is the gravest of all disorders, graver than concupiscence of the eyes and of the flesh, graver than avarice and excessive love of riches and luxury. We are dealing, in fact, with a disturbance and perversion of the superior parts of the soul and its most elevated faculties, reason and will, which command all the rest. "The corruption of the best is the worst." For the worst corruption is that which perverts the most exalted and profound that is in us. This is the spiritual disorder that exists in the Devil, who can know neither avarice nor lust, but who refuses to serve and obey God, insisting, "I will not serve!"

Such a love of absolute independence disturbs our judgment, hinders us in understanding our duty and perverts the will under the pretense of making us free, equal to God and independent like Him. This is, evidently, the great aim of the modern world which rebels against the Church. While it agrees to fight against avarice, seeking to better the lot of the poor and to repress its own coarser instincts, it wishes, nevertheless, to do all it does by itself, without the help of God. The world intends, mainly, to obey reason alone and not God.

Although the modern world may be described as rationalistic, it disobeys reason rather than obey God. This pretended absolute independence pushes it into all types of slavery and the worst type of tyranny: that of rebellious passions and unjust laws passed without any recourse to conscience. Such legislation is aimed at the self-interest of the party in power, against which there remains no possibility of vindication since absolute and eternal justice is rejected, and the rights of God are repudiated!

General obedience to the commandments of God and His Church is the sole efficacious remedy for this anarchy and tyranny. Man must understand that God, being his Creator, has a sovereign right over him; he must understand that his intelligence and his will were created only to know, love, and serve God, and thus to obtain eternal life and supreme beatitude.

We must acknowledge, then, that the Lord is our Master and that it is our duty to obey Him. Besides, His law does not produce violence but proceeds from His love and produces love. It is true folly to rebel against that which alone can lead us to happiness!

This general obedience frees us already from the main slavery of the world. He who obeys God understands, then, that in the final analysis he cannot and must not obey any other than God and His representatives, spiritual and temporal. How could he really obey men who are his equals? He clearly sees that he must never obey a human law that is contrary to the law of God, and that a human law has no authority except insofar as it is based on divine law and springs from it.

But this general obedience is insufficient for some souls. The commandments of God and the Church lay down for us the way that leads to Heaven, but there are different ways, more or less perfect, of practicing the commandments of the Lord, of loving Him with all our heart and of loving our neighbor. These commandments lay down only the general outline, precisely that they may be applicable to all. However, when an individual soul seeks to know exactly what God demands of it in a determined circumstance, the matter is not so simple. One runs the risk of being mistaken and letting oneself be invaded by the spirit of the world, by its prejudices and maxims.

It would be a great grace if Our Lord came in person to tell us: "Here is precisely what I want of you today at such an hour, and what I want of you tomorrow; and this is what you ought to prepare yourself for on the day after tomorrow." And sometimes the Lord has even done this with certain saints: to St. Catherine of Siena, for example, He directly gave His orders and He Himself guided her in all the particulars of her life.

What Our Lord did directly with some saints, He does with all His religious by means of their superiors. In making the vow of obedience, the religious makes a contract with the Lord: "All the orders of my superiors that will not be contrary to Your holy laws I shall consider as an order given by You, as by a divine word." The Lord responds: "You will have in exchange the holy liberty of the sons of God, you will be freed from all slavery of the world." In brief, this is the meaning of holy obedience.

Such obedience has been strongly criticized by Naturalism, even more than the other vows. Naturalism has maintained that the cause of all our weaknesses is lack of personality; but this attitude betrays a false concept of religious obedience. To maintain its thesis, Naturalism has wished to consider only the negative aspect of holy obedience, that is, the separation it demands. If it had considered what it has that is positive, that is, the consecration that assures full conformity of our will to the will of God, then it would have recognized both that there is no personality more wonderful than that of the saints, and that this is the fruit of their obedience.

To comprehend well the true nature of holy obedience, it must be considered, as with the other vows, under its two aspects of separation and consecration.

Separation

Holy poverty and holy chastity involve, as we have said, the mortification of the body, the senses, and the heart. Holy obedience involves above all the mortification of one's own will and one's own judgment. Thus, it can be rightly affirmed that the three vows organize in a permanent way both the interior and exterior mortifications.

We know well the dangers deriving from our self-will. St. Catherine of Siena has repeatedly insisted on this subject. One's self-will is that which is not conformed to the will of God. It is the source of sin, the act which separates us from God. St. Bernard says that if self-will is suppressed, hell will no longer have reason to exist. But self-will is dangerous especially because it can ruin all our actions. What is best in us becomes reprehensible when it is mixed with that will which seeks itself as an end instead of subordinating itself to God.

If God finds self-will present in an act of mortification, for example in fasting, it is not accepted by Him; if He sees self-will as the basis of a sacrifice, the sacrifice is none other than a lie and an abomination to Him. Such is the value of every act done out of pride—work done that it may be seen by the eyes of men. Now we can see that the vow of obedience assures the mortification of this dangerous will that diverts us from salvation.

In the religious life, it is not enough to obey exteriorly, with an obedience of action; the adhesion of the will is required. It is necessary to subject our will to that of the superior (*cf.* Bourdaloue). In fact, exterior obedience or obedience of action without the adhering of the will is only a slavish obedience, that of a slave, of a servant who is only obligated to do exteriorly what is commanded him.

Our obedience ought to be the obedience of a son and a friend. "I no longer call you servants, but friends." Indeed, we did not enter the monastery to place ourselves under an external discipline, as in a barracks; we came to conform our will to the will of God.

"An obedience that is merely external, without the subjection of the will, has no value in the eyes of God. It is the letter, the body of obedience but this body is only a corpse if the spirit does not give it life" (Bourdaloue). Exterior obedience, or obedience of action, is none other than servitude if adhesion of the will is lacking. It does not become a virtue unless it is directed by the will in free submission to the will of God. When an order that is repugnant to our nature is received, external obedience becomes a virtue if our will freely immolates itself to the will of God. St. Gregory was able to say that this sacrifice is greater than all those of the Old Law, because at that time only victims were immolated while now we immolate our will.

This submission of the will ought to be manifested externally in three ways: it ought to be *prompt, universal,* and *without distinction of person.*

It ought to be *prompt.* This derives from the honor and dignity of him who commands. The higher the dignity of him who commands, the greater the offense caused by slowness in carrying out the orders. Obedience, to be perfect, ought to anticipate, in a certain sense, the order and respond promptly to it.

Once, when the provincials of our order asked the religious of their convents to depart for the missions, all wished to depart though knowing that they would be going to meet death. Those who were able to go wept with joy, and those who, because of their duties, could not, cried because they were hindered from following their brethren in giving testimony with their blood.

Obedience ought to be *universal* and without limits—both in great and in little things, however easy or difficult they may be, whether practical or, in some way, impractical. "What I am subtracting from the act," you might say, "is nothing." And, in fact, it is nothing considered in itself. But, as constituent part of an order given by God it becomes respectable and holy. If you do not do it, you are taking away a part of the sacrifice that ought to be offered in its totality to God, and God, as Isaias says "hates in a special way the sacrilegious robbery of part of a holocaust" (Isa. 61:8). On the other hand, He will have His faithful servant who obeyed in little things enter into Heaven: "You have shown you can be faithful in small things, I will trust you with greater; come and join in your master's happiness" (Mt. 25:21).

Obedience should be made *without distinction of person.* In other words, it is necessary to obey all superiors, whoever they may be—lovable or less lovable, prudent or impulsive, holy or less perfect—because through the word of the one or of another it is always God who speaks. We have made the vow to obey God, not a creature!

To obey a person because he is congenial to us, and not to do this when he ceases to be, is no longer obedience to God, and is not at all meritorious. The saints, who never neglect the mortification of their own will, tell us: "Tremble when your superior commands what agrees with your nature, because it could happen that the principal motive of your act is its natural attraction, and then the fruit of obedience is lost."

It is useless, in fact, to follow our own desires; it is necessary to adhere to the will of our superior, that is, to the will of God. We should rejoice, then, when what is commanded us is contrary to our nature, because then the sacrifice of our will is much more certain, much purer, and more excellent. So let us prefer a superior who opposes us, and tests us, a superior firm and severe, to another more moderate and more indulgent. St. John of the Cross, gravely ill and nearly dying, had the possibility of choosing between two monasteries. In one the prior was his friend; in the other, a bitter enemy. John of the Cross chose the latter. Certainly, it is not necessary to act like this great saint, but we all ought to be scrupulously careful so as not to lose the merit of obedience.

"If someone by every sort of solicitation and secret intrigue, induces his superior to do what he wishes and to confer on him a certain office, this is not done in obedience," says St. Bernard, "because in such a case it is not you who are obeying a superior, but a superior who is obeying you. Both will have to answer before God, even if you should succeed in your office because God does not judge on the basis of your success, but on the basis of your conformity to His will." "Concern over success," says Bourdaloue with respect to this question, "is a concern that ought to be left to divine Providence; what ought to be of concern to us is to do our duty, that is, to obey."

Interior submission of the will, however, is not enough. It is still necessary to sacrifice one's own judgment, one's reason, the highest part of oneself. And it is only thus that our sacrifice merits the name of holocaust. The holocaust was the most perfect sacrifice because the totality of the victim was offered to God: all was consumed in the fire, even to total destruction. The same must happen in the interior sacrifice of holy obedience. For obedience to be perfect, it is not enough to submit the will; it is also necessary to submit one's judgment to that of one's legitimately constituted superior who commands rightly. Without this submission of judgment, obedience runs the risk of losing all the qualities required to constitute its value. It runs the risk of being neither generous, nor prompt, nor universal. In addition, it loses sight of the fact that basically it is God who is commanding.

If this submission of our own judgment is refused, the spirit of criticism will not delay in making us completely lose the merit of our acts and, at the same time, in introducing the spirit of division into the community. If someone assumes the right of censoring all that does not please him, it is certain that for him there can be no true obedience. If, on the other hand, a religious obeys solely because it seems that the given order is reasonable—if he submits because of human reasons—he or she is certainly not performing an act of obedience. Similarly, one would not be making an act of faith in admitting the existence of God as a result of a rational demonstration.

Holy obedience (I do not say all types of obedience, but holy obedience) involves the submission of will and judgment to the will and judgment of God as expressed by our superior. "Then," you may say, "obedience ought to be blind. But how can we renounce those lights that make us rational beings?" The masters of the spiritual life respond: "Yes, obedience ought to be blind. It is enough to be certain that the given order is not sinful, or contrary to the divine law or the expressed order of a higher authority. We have made this contract with God: All that is commanded me by my legitimate superior and is not contrary to your law, I oblige myself to consider as a divine word, as a divine order."

To satisfy the legitimate needs of reason, it is enough to be assured that the order comes from God. Once this is established, holy obedience ought to be blind like that of Abraham who, at the Lord's command, prepared to immolate his son, Isaac. "Religious obedience is sufficient for salvation when it submits itself to the rule *(secundum regulam)* in obligatory things, and it is perfect when it submits in things permitted; it would be imprudent if it induced our soul to submit to illicit things" *(S. T.* II-II, q. 104, a. 5 ad 3).

The same is true for holy obedience as for supernatural faith. Supernatural faith is, in a certain sense, blind; it is enough to know that the obscure mystery proposed to us comes from God. It is a happy blindness, immensely superior to clearness of reason, because this night of faith and humble obedience diffuses its own light—that of the gifts of wisdom and understanding. "And night is my illumination in my delight." The obedient religious can say: "This night becomes for me a light wholly divine and fills me with joy, giving me certainty that I am fulfilling the will of God."

"But," say others, "sometimes it happens that what is commanded us is absurd and obviously imprudent, committing us to work evidently destined for failure." It can be answered: "You are unaware of many reasons that can motivate the given order; sometimes there are a hundred matters pertaining to the general welfare about which you know nothing; you are not in a position to judge, since you do not have the grace of state as do your superiors. Moreover, it may be that your superior wishes to and ought to test the quality of your obedience. Finally, it may be that the given order, considered in itself, is imprudent and comes from a prejudice or defect of our superior; yet, it is still not contrary to divine law." Does this order, then, come from God? Yes, certainly; God often leaves defects in superiors to keep them humble and to test the subjects.

The thing commanded, considered in itself, may be imprudent and inopportune; but holy obedience does not command you to approve of it as such, or to continue to have it practiced if later you become superiors. Judge, then, the thing commanded for what it is in itself. However, convince yourself also that it is commanded you by God, and tell yourself that at that moment it is for you what is better, more reasonable, indeed the only reasonable thing to do.

They command you, perhaps, to interrupt your prayer to do some manual work that could also be done later, as happened often to St. Margaret Mary. But, it is the voice of God that is speaking. There is nothing better for you. Your superior can make a mistake, but you will never make a mistake: you will immolate not only your will, but also your judgment. This is what God commands you. Do not be anxious about success; it is up to divine Providence to take care of that, and it will not fail to do so.

Finally, if there is some inconvenience that is notable and, above all, seemingly contrary to the general welfare, you are not forbidden humbly to submit your difficulties to your superior. Open your soul to him after you have prayed, reflected and purified your intention. This simplicity enhances your obedience. If your superior persists, do not doubt that the better thing for you is to obey. Such is the twofold mortification of will and judgment that holy obedience involves.

Consecration

But this twofold mortification has as its end the consecration of our will and judgment to God, their identification in some way with the will and judgment of God, and our consequent liberation from all the slaveries of the world. Certainly general obedience, by conforming our will to that of God, frees us from the obligation of submitting to unjust laws, enables us to reign over our passions, over the world, whose maxims and vain attractions we despise, and over the Devil, whose temptations we repulse.

And if it is true to say of obedience in general that "to serve God is to reign," with greater reason this can be said of religious obedience. Religious obedience, assuring the full conformity of our will to the divine will, perfectly frees us from all the slaveries of the world. It especially frees us from ourselves and from our passions and prejudices. These would hinder our freedom to direct ourselves toward the truly good things, to make us free as God Himself, dependent on Him alone and independent of all else.

A Catholic orator once said that the vow of obedience is the Tabor of the will, the glorious manifestation of a human freedom identified with divine freedom. Our Lord did not intend anything other than this when He promised us "the holy freedom of the sons of God," the freedom to run on the path of the good and along the road of perfection for which liberty is made. The vow is, therefore, a sovereignly free act of love for the good, and of contempt and hatred for all that is contrary to the good.

St. Catherine of Siena says that the truly obedient are the children that Jesus spoke of when He said, "Let the little ones come to Me, because theirs is the Kingdom of Heaven." Whoever does not humble himself as a child in the simplicity of obedience will not enter the Kingdom of Heaven; he will remain a slave of his passions, a slave of the world, of the Devil, of his will and of his prejudices.

Together with this liberation, holy obedience offers us the joy of being able to say even here below: "I am doing all that

God wills, and can do nothing better." It is the joy of doing one's duty even in the smallest acts. The value of each act is great, so that even recreation and sleep are sanctified, since they are commanded by God and we take them only for the love of God. What is there more secure than obedience? Even the Psalmist exclaims: "Yes, I love Your commandments more than gold, than purest gold" (Ps. 119:127).

Besides the joy of feeling ourselves on the path that leads to God, holy obedience gives us the strength and boldness of the saints. And in this case also, the hundredfold is received; our will, for having renounced itself, has become strong from the very strength of God. Modernism speaks of initiative, but forgets that the true initiative, that which bears fruit in the supernatural order, is born of obedience.

The obedient religious applies himself to learning what God wishes from him. Once he finds out, nothing stops him. He can attempt what is humanly impossible because the grace of God is with him. Hence our blessed father St. Dominic sent his sons to all parts of the world, saying to them: "Go on foot, without money, without anxieties for tomorrow, begging your food; and I promise you that, despite difficulties and want, you will never lack what is necessary."

How many times the divine power has miraculously come to place itself at the service of obedience! The Lord was pleased to recall these examples to St. Catherine of Siena: "Have you not read in Sacred Scripture that many, not to transgress the order of God, threw themselves in flames, and the flames did them no harm? So it was with the three children thrown in the furnace, and so with many others I could mention. The water became solid under the feet of St. Maurus when, out of obedience, he went to save a religious who was drowning. He did not think of himself. He thought, in the light of faith, of performing an order he had received. He went over the water as if he were walking on land, and he saved the religious" *(Dial.* chap. 165).

Finally, obedience, conforming our judgment to the judgment of God, makes us wiser than the wisest of the world. The Psalmist can say: "How much subtler than my teachers, through my meditating on Your decrees! How much more perceptive than the elders, as a result of my respecting Your precepts!" (Ps. 119:98 ff.) The humble novice in his obedience is more intelligent and prudent than the so-called incredulous who confide in themselves. Obedience frees us at the same time from the influence of the judgments of men and liberates us from our prejudices, from our scruples, and from our bewilderment. If our conduct is criticized, with all security and humility we can let others say what they wish. God is with us.

It is certainly possible to compare holy obedience to the Holy Eucharist. In the one as well as in the other, the Word is certainly present, hidden under earthly or human appearances: in the Eucharist, hidden under the species of bread and wine; in the order of our superior, hidden under the appearance of a human person. In the one case as in the other, the Word comes to enlighten us, to strengthen us, to draw us tenderly to Himself and assimilate us to Himself.

We should learn to obey in the light of faith, just as we receive Holy Communion in the light of faith. We should learn to see God always in the person of our superiors, to recognize the signal of God in the bell that calls us. Thus, day by day, our will will die and eventually lose itself in the will of God that is infinitely holy, free, strong, and blessed. Day by day our judgment will also die and give way to that spirit of wisdom, understanding, and counsel that little by little transforms our meditation into contemplation and nourishes our charity with a food more and more divine.

Thus, through mortification and renunciation we will attain the light of union with God. The daily practice of the religious life will lead us to the goal of all spiritual life: toward a more and more intimate contemplation and an increasingly ardent love for God.

CHAPTER XI

The Cross

*If anyone wants to be a follower of Mine,
let him renounce himself and take up his
cross and follow Me—Matthew 16:24*

WE have reflected on the necessity of active mortification in our life and on the value of mortification organized in a permanent way in the religious life through the practice of the three vows. Our Lord alluded to this when He said: "Let him renounce himself"; but He also added: "and take up his cross." It is not enough, then to deny ourselves and mortify ourselves. We must also carry patiently the cross that the Lord gives us for purifying ourselves and saving souls.

That which we call "the cross" in Christian terminology (by analogy with the sufferings and death of our divine Master) are the physical and moral sufferings of daily life which arise from our relationship to the exterior world and to those around us. They are especially those sent to us directly by God in order to purify us and save souls. Like the Cross imposed on Jesus by His Father, they are the price of our salvation. "He was humbler yet, even to accepting death, death on a cross" (Phil. 2:8).

The necessity of the cross in Christian life is due to the fact that we carry somewhere within ourselves the seeds of a profound evil, but we do not know exactly where these principles of death are to be found. Even when we are mortified and have made every effort to be regular and fervent in the religious life, a great number of unconscious defects remain in us: spiritual sensuality and spiritual pride, attachment to one's own judgment and will, etc. All of these hinder us from being what we ought to be— living images of Jesus Christ. What an abyss between a religious who is simply ordinary and one who is a saint! This abyss is bridged by the cross born in patience.

Our Lord knows better than we where evil is harbored within us. Wishing to heal us, He sends us His messengers to admonish us, and He Himself sets the iron to our wounds to extract all the sources of corruption from them. Even if we were not sick, He would send the cross to detach us from affections that are certainly legitimate, but which hinder us from becoming totally supernatural.

Finally, He sends us the cross that we may be of help to Him as instruments of redemption. If we wish to save souls, we must use the same means that Our Lord used. Christ appeared to St. Rose of Lima on the day of her investiture under the guise of a sculptor and asked her to help Him work a block of marble. The saint replied that she knew only how to weave and cook. Then Our Lord let her understand that that block of marble, still unformed and rough, was she herself, and that she ought to have patience and let herself be worked and smoothed so as to become the image of her divine Master, a precious stone in the eternal city of souls.

The necessity of the cross is proportionate to the level of glory to which God wishes to lead us. Some people that we wrongly and with a sense of compassion call "tormented souls," live in the midst of almost continual sufferings because Our Lord wishes to lead them much higher than others that are not tormented but easily contented. "The more God loves us," say all the saints, "the heavier the crosses that He sends us."

Patience is the virtue of the saints (*cf.* St. Teresa and Tauler). "Life to me, of course, is Christ, but then death would bring me something more" (Phil. 1:21).

The spiritual life does not acquire a definite intensity without a profound death, which God alone can produce in us.

To bear the cross patiently we must have an understanding of it and see its purpose. Hence, it is not useless to know the different ways by which God tries individuals to purify them. There are some crosses that have for their purpose the purification of our *sensibility* and its complete submission to the spirit. Such crosses are frequent and common to many persons, especially to beginners. There are others that are heavier and have for their purpose the full purification of our *spirit* and its submission to God. These are given only to a small number already advanced in the interior life.

Crosses of Sensibility

One of the greatest imperfections of beginners is spiritual sensuality and spiritual pride. We are attached inordinately to the sensible sweetness that we find in devotion, seeking it as an end and not as a simple means of going to God. We boast of our perfection and judge others very severely. We put on airs like masters, while we remain only poor beginners.

Our Lord finds it necessary to wean us, to take away the milk of sensible consolations in order to give us a more substantial food, a more spiritual food. Our sensibility then finds only aridity and desolation. And thus we become also more humble, no longer judging others with such severity, and not putting on airs like masters.

This aridity should never throw us into discouragement, for if it is accompanied by detachment from the world and by habitual recollection of God, it is a proof, says St. John of the Cross, that it does not come from our lukewarmness. Rather, it is a gain for us: "For me to live is Christ, and to die is gain." This cross teaches us to serve God for Himself, with unselfishness, and it preserves us from the illusions of the Devil.

To purify our sensibility, God dispenses other crosses also. He can send us sicknesses, deprive us of a friendship that perhaps absorbed us beyond measure, take away certain honors, or an office, for example, that seemed due us. But above all He despoils us of the goods on which we had concentrated our affection, and mercifully comes to ask us for this part of our love that we had not thought of giving Him. When this emptying is insufficient, He mercifully permits little or great persecutions on the part of men, and the temptations of the Devil.

Yet what are the little crosses we have to carry in comparison to those of the saints? We should recall our great St. Peter Martyr who was visited in his cell by some saintly women. For this he was accused in the chapter[1] of an infamous offense which he had not committed. The saint did not wish to reveal the Heavenly graces with which he was favored and so he listened to the severe reproach of his prior without speaking a word. He was banished from the priory in Bologna and relegated to Iesi in the zone of Le Marche. The infamy weighed heavily upon him, gravely dishonoring him. The saint complained to the Lord. One day, prostrate at the foot of his crucifix, with his eyes flooded with tears, he exclaimed: "My Jesus, You know my innocence. How can You permit such a false accusation to dishonor my reputation?" The voice from the crucifix answered: "Was I not abandoned to opprobrium and overwhelmed with insults despite My innocence? Learn from My example to bear the harshest calumnies!" From that day onward, St. Peter Martyr understood through experience the mystery of the Cross and all its splendors. From that humiliation, which was a visit from

---

1 Editor's note: A chapter is a gathering of members in a religious congregation to pray and discuss matters important to the congregation.

God, he learned much more than from the Heavenly favors of those holy visitors who were the cause of that humiliation.

When what we are and what we have done for the community is not acknowledged, when our good intentions are misunderstood, we should remember St. Benedict Labre. A coadjutor of the Society of Jesus who was struck by the fervor of that poor man of Christ, wished to meet and talk with him, but the latter withdrew himself. Every testimony of sympathy wounded the humility of his soul. On the other hand, when some urchins threw refuse upon him and treated him as a fool, he slowed his pace and even stopped, to savor this mortification. At times certain young ruffians were not content with insults. One day two of them threw him to the ground and, after pulling his beard and hair, trampled on him and spat in his face. The saint did not seek to defend himself or free himself. Some passers-by, becoming indignant, drove off the young delinquents. "He is a fool," they said. "Why shouldn't we have fun with him?" "You are the fools," a woman courageously replied. "He is a saint." The poor man of Christ had become a fool, a fool of the divine foolishness of the Cross, which is supreme wisdom in the eyes of God.

The crosses that we have to bear are much lighter, because we are not called to such an exalted level of sanctity. We ought to have the humility of not asking God for crosses superior to our strength, but of bearing patiently those the Lord sends us, those He asks us to bear. Jesus has said to all: "If you wish to follow Me, deny yourself and carry your cross."

The cross that purifies our sensibility by elevating it and subjecting it more and more perfectly to the spirit, helps us to know ourselves better. It reveals to us our unworthiness and weakness, teaches us to despise ourselves and consider ourselves, as St. Paul suggests, inferior to others. It teaches us, also, to know God better, no longer through sensible consolations but through tribulations. As a result, it is no longer the Jesus of the manger, but He on the Cross, who reveals Himself to us through our own experience. Thus we begin truly to love God, who is purely spiritual, and the exigencies of His love, which is purely spiritual. Doing this our whole being becomes spiritualized.

Crosses of the Spirit

There are other still heavier crosses that weigh only on those individuals much advanced in the interior life. These are crosses that it is good to know about—not that we may ask the Lord for them, but that we may see how far we are from the summits of love and how foolish our spiritual pride is when it wishes to make us believe that we are advanced in the way of perfection.

The Holy Spirit Himself has judged it useful to reveal these terrible crosses to all in the incomparable book of Job. These alone enable us to comprehend the sense of certain exclamations of Our Lord on Calvary. From such crosses we also learn what kind of sufferings await us in purgatory.

The *purpose* of these crosses is not so much to spiritualize our sensibility, as to supernaturalize our spirit. These crosses serve to detach the spirit from itself and to subject it to God in such a way that it is transformed, so to speak, into Him in the same way that wood, becoming prey to the fire, warms and illumines like the fire (St. John of the Cross). These crosses of the spirit, sent directly by God, make the superior part of the soul suffer. The *means* God uses to purify us is a supernatural light, so living and so intense that the eyes of the soul, still not strong enough to bear it, are dazzled and blinded by it, experiencing an acute suffering from it, as happens to the owl that is dazzled and blinded by too much sunlight.

But this mysterious divine light, though it is blinding, makes one see. First of all it makes the soul see what it is in reality, showing it the unsuspected depths of its misery. Then, in contrast, it reveals God in His transcendence and infinite purity. This revelation is in a manner so entirely new, though very obscure, that the soul seems bedazzled, no longer seeing the relationship between this knowledge and that which it formerly enjoyed. Although it is elevated by its labors toward the light, it seems to the person that it is more and more engulfed by the night.

Now we shall see how Our Lord purifies, in this painful ascent, the humility of the saints, their faith, their hope, and their charity, that is, the virtues proper to the higher degrees of the soul and spirit. In this way we shall discover how superficial and imperfect our humility, faith, hope, and charity still are.

God teaches humility directly to the saints, revealing Himself to them, showing them the abyss that separates them from Him. We should also learn humility by contemplating the life of the saints and measuring the abyss that separates us from them.

Humility is the basis of the whole spiritual edifice. In order that a structure may be solid and lasting, it is necessary that the foundation be very deep. The foundation stone of the whole spiritual edifice is faith. Almost all of us are now content to place this stone on the ground and to build on top of it; but this is not enough—the edifice will not endure. At times we understand very clearly that it is necessary to excavate deeply; and yet we are content to hardly scratch the surface, so that after some years in the religious life the edifice is barely more solid than at the beginning, and a storm is enough to destroy the whole. Consequently, it is necessary to excavate deeply. Humility does this.

When Our Lord wishes to build a tall spiritual edifice in a person, He Himself looks to the excavating, and to such a depth that we do not even suspect. The dazzling supernatural fight with which God blinds the individual reveals to it its miseries, its weaknesses, and its poverty.

It sees that in itself it is nothing, and that by itself it can do nothing but err, sin, and return to nothingness. Bl. Angela of Foligno saw herself as an abyss of sin. At the same time the soul feels unable to do anything whatsoever for its own salvation. It has the impression that all it undertakes fails, while others are succeeding. It seems to it that, instead of advancing, it is going backwards.

One day St. Benedict Labre began his confession with these words: "Father, I am a great sinner; help me make a good confession." The confessor, who did not know him, believed that he was dealing with a contrite sinner and began to encourage him. But in all that Benedict Labre said to him, he found no sin. He thought that the man did not know how to make a confession and so he asked a few questions on the Decalogue; but the very profound answers he received made him understand that he had a saint before him.

St. Dominic scourged himself every night for his sins. These saints, however much Our Lord eventually exalted them, did not become proud; they experienced their own misery.

After having taught His saints by means of the cross to become meek and humble of heart, in His likeness, the Lord began to purify their faith. Faith is the virtue that consists in believing whatever God has revealed solely because God has revealed it. In fact, this is precisely the reason why we do believe even though there are also many other secondary motives that make the act of faith easier. For instance, we believe also because we experience in ourselves the action of God through the consolations He gives us and through the progress He has us make, or because the things we undertake for Him succeed, or because we see the harmony of the dogmas with one another and with the great natural truths.

But let us suppose that God takes from us all these secondary motives so that we no longer experience His action in us. We feel nothing but aridity and desolation and we succeed in nothing we undertake, as happened to St. Dominic at Fanjeaux. Let us suppose that the harmony of doctrine disappears and gives way to a profound obscurity. Nothing remains any longer except the single motive of belief: God has spoken it and confirmed it with His miracles.

In this way Our Lord tries the faith of His saints to purify it. The supernatural lights that He sends and with which He renders the dogmas luminous in an unexpected way, blinds them. Since they were formerly accustomed to believe in a rather superficial way, they now feel bewildered and even come to ask themselves whether they have not lost their faith. On this point Our Lord also permits temptations of the Devil.

Bl. Henry Suso had to undergo a temptation of this type for ten years. St. Vincent de Paul, who offered himself to save the soul of a poor priest, was so tempted on this point that he asked himself whether he would not end up by denying his faith. No longer successful in discerning whether he consented or not to the temptation, he put a pin in his sleeve, saying: "When I make the external action of drawing out this pin, I shall no longer believe." In the meantime, in the purity of his clouded faith and despite all the difficulties and objections, he believed with all his strength because of this one motive: "God has spoken it." He thus completed the painful immolation of his intelligence to the obscure divine word, and this act introduced him to a new world. Is it not necessary that the sun go down in order that the stars may be seen? In the same way, the habitual light of our reason must be extinguished so that pure faith may become the resplendent night that Sacred Scripture speaks of: "And night is my illumination in my delights."

After the purification of faith follows that of hope. Hope is the virtue that makes us desire to attain and possess God by trusting in His help. In reality, to attain Heaven and to live our religious life we trust in God—that is the principal motive of hope. But we also trust in ourselves, in our virtues, in the success of our works, in our friends and in the help of our superiors. Yet, if God suddenly took away from us these human helps—our friends, affections, the esteem of our superiors—if He revealed to us our miseries and our weakness, would we still hope in Him?

We should recall the example of St. John the Baptist, who, having announced the coming of the Kingdom of God, was abandoned by all in his prison and saw the triumph of the wicked. Do you think that he did not have to fight against discouragement? St. John of the Cross almost abandoned the work of reforming Carmel when in his prison he asked himself whether in the final analysis his persecutors were not right in opposing him. Bl. Angela of Foligno asked herself whether she had not given way to the temptation of despair.

The saints hoped against every human hope because of this one motive: God is infinitely powerful and good. It is not He who abandons us first; He always wishes to raise us up again from our offenses when our soul cries to Him. Thus Jesus purifies in the crucible of pain the hope of His most intimate friends.

After hope it is charity's turn. Charity is the supreme virtue which makes us love God for Himself alone, because He is infinitely good and because He loved us first (*cf.* 1 Jn. 4:10). This is the principal motive for which we love God. Yet, we also find many other secondary motives. For example, He gives us what we ask for, draws us to Himself, and makes the work undertaken for Him succeed.

But if we had to love God in desolation, in obscurity, in the privation of all sensible and spiritual consolations; if we had to continue to love Him effectively, to accomplish all our duties and persevere in prayer only because He is infinitely good and died for us on the Cross, would we have the strength to make this sublime act of charity? When nothing any longer arises for the soul except bitterness, both from God and from men; when one is reduced to the same state as Our Lord when He exclaimed on the Cross, "My God, My God, why have You forsaken Me?" then it is that the soul's act of love saves the world and it becomes, in a certain sense, co-redemptrix like the Sorrowful Mother. What incomparable grandeur of the saints, and how far we are from these summits!

Consider the sailor's wife who does not stop thinking of her husband although he no longer sends any word that he is alive. She continues to love him in her sorrow as if he were present, not wishing to love anyone else, bringing up her children to love their father. If we admire her, how much more ought we to admire and love the bride of Christ who—like St. Rose of Lima, St. Teresa, St. Mary Magdalen de Pazzi—remains fifteen or twenty years waiting for Jesus Christ to return to her soul, never ceasing to think of Him and to love Him with a love as strong as it is sorrowful. And all for the single motive that Jesus is infinitely good and died for us on the Cross!

How to Carry the Cross

From what we have said, we can develop the doctrine on the way to carry the cross. You, holy ones, brides of Christ, bring us to understand this mystery of the cross and the place it ought to occupy in our life.

We know that we should not ask the Lord for crosses that He judges inopportune to send us because of our weakness. We know that we should not despise the small crosses, since the great ones can make us proud. We know that it is not enough to admire the crosses of the saints, and also that there is nothing more unsupportable than to put on airs of being martyrs when in reality we are not.

We should, then, dismiss these deplorable illusions. We should no longer complain of suffering from the faults of others when we make others suffer even more. We should learn to bear the crosses that the Lord sends us: not those that are pleasing to us, but those pleasing to Him. We must teach ourselves to bear them with resignation, love, and gratitude.

With resignation. It is indeed necessary to suffer. Modern progress, which seeks to suppress the cross like those "enemies of the cross" of whom St. Paul speaks (Phil. 3:18), will never attain what it desires. Even if it did manage to diminish pain in the physical order, what can it do in the moral order? It is necessary to suffer. If we vex ourselves like the bad thief, our irritation will only increase our suffering. Our Lord asks us to allow Him to work—to allow Him to work to reproduce His image in us.

With love. Our Lord does not ask us to love suffering in itself, but to love it as a means of salvation, just as a very bitter medicine that will give us back our health can be loved. We are not asked to feel this love in a sensible way, but to give proof of it by persevering, despite tribulations, in the practice of our religious duties, especially prayer. Jesus expects us to turn to him with ardent prayer, because He has already decided to hear us and to lead us much higher than we ourselves could desire. Therefore, we should love the cross for the love of souls and gladly accept being associated with Our Lord in His work of redemption.

With gratitude. The cross is necessary for us. The Lord tries us only because He loves us, because He wishes to assimilate us to Himself, to spiritualize our sensibility, to supernaturalize our spirit, to give us a more exalted knowledge of ourselves and of Him, and also to give us a stronger love.

The active life is necessary but the cross is even more needed because through the cross our passive purification, under the action of God, is accomplished—and the action of God is much more fruitful than our own. Together with humility, the cross develops in us the three virtues which are properly divine and are the heart of the Christian life: faith, hope, and charity. The cross makes our soul similar to the soul of Christ, and therefore similar to God.

Sometimes this effect of the cross is so sublime that it is reflected in the human body. St. Benedict Labre was passing through the streets of Rome one day when an artist, who had visited all the museums of Italy without finding what he was searching for, stopped him. He begged the saint to follow him and led him to his room. There, after he had painted the resemblance of the poor man of Christ, the artist knelt down, kissed his hands and exclaimed, "You have the face of Christ!"

On another occasion, the poor saint was seen enveloped by a brilliant light. Emanating from his face were rays that shone with such a splendor that he seemed to be on fire. Such was the fruit of the cross in the soul of this saint. For such crosses the angels envy us, being unable to give God this testimony of love. The cross leads all Christians to the true light of God, the prelude to Heaven: *Per crucem ad lucem* (Through the Cross to the Light).

CHAPTER XII

The Efficacy of Prayer

The Father will give you anything you ask
Him in My name—John 15:17

AFTER we considered the necessity of mortification and the cross, both to purify us from all affection for things of the world and for ourselves, and also to spiritualize our sensibility and supernaturalize our spirit, we then examined how the cross purifies our humility, our faith, our hope, and our charity.

This purification is essentially destined to make us know and love God better. By means of this knowledge and love union with God is realized. In fact, Our Lord, after having told us, "If anyone wishes to come after Me, let him deny himself, take up his cross and follow Me," added, "Whoever follows Me does not walk in darkness, but will have the light of life."

Necessity of Prayer

This knowledge and this love of God are attained in an immediate way in the diverse forms of prayer, especially in mental prayer. In order to possess a living faith that operates through charity, in order to ignite and increase that fire of charity with which we must inflame ourselves, communication with God is indispensable. We enter into this communication with God through habitual meditation on religious truths and by means of mental prayer.

Indeed, we know only that which we thoroughly examine and meditate upon. Since we love only what we know, we continue to love only the things that we do not cease to think about. Time and distance weaken and eventually extinguish the most intense affections. If we never think of God, if our spirit remains far from Him, we shall no longer love Him.

What kind of attraction can be offered a believer by the beauty of the truths of our faith—such as the Most Holy Trinity, the Incarnation, the Redemption, the Eucharist, the holiness of the Blessed Virgin—if he knows these truths only superficially and has never seriously meditated on them and savored them in depth?

Mental Prayer and Mortification

We should note that mortification prepares for mental prayer, and that the latter, in its turn, facilitates mortification. Therefore, prayer and mortification influence one another. Mortification and patience prepare for prayer through the purification and detachment they produce in us. They enable the person to take flight toward God, and this flight is prayer itself.

At the same time, prayer enables us to carry our cross in the light. It reminds us of the reason for this cross, makes us carry it with love, and obtains from God the grace of resignation. Thus, prayer and mortification give each other reciprocal help. Prayer is superior, however, just as union with God is superior to detachment from the world. Indeed, we detach ourselves from the world to unite ourselves with God, but we do not seek union with God to detach ourselves from the world.

Efficacy of Prayer

We must move on, now, to speak of the efficacy of prayer and the source of this efficacy. In the first place, we ask ourselves: Do we truly believe in the efficacy of prayer? This is certainly a question that concerns all people without distinction. It touches not only those that are beginning and those that have realized great progress, but also those in the state of mortal sin because the sinner, even if he has lost sanctifying grace and hence can no longer merit, can, nevertheless, pray. Merit that has a right to compensation refers to divine justice;[1] prayer, on the other hand, is directed to divine mercy which often hears and lifts up, without any merit, the individuals fallen into the state of spiritual death.

From the profound abyss into which he has fallen, the most miserable man can send up towards God's mercy that cry which is called prayer. The beggar, who possesses only his poverty, can pray in the name of his misery and, if he places all his heart in this supplication, he compels mercy to bow down toward him because the abyss of misery calls to the abyss of mercy. The soul rises again, and God is glorified.

We should recall the conversion of Mary Magdalen. Also remember the prayer of Daniel for Israel: "Lord! We have sinned, we have committed iniquity; departing from You we merit all Your punishments. But for the glory of Your name, pardon us, O Lord!" (Dan. 3:28–35) The psalms are full of these supplications: "Help us, God our savior, . . . blot out our sins, rescue us" (Ps. 79:9). "You, my refuge and shield, I put my hope in your word" (Ps. 119:114).

Do we believe in the power of prayer? When temptation threatens to make us fall, when the light is extinguished in us, when the cross is difficult to carry, do we have recourse to prayer as Our Lord taught us? Or does it happen that we doubt—if not in theory at least in practice—the efficacy of prayer? And yet we well know the promise of Our Lord: "Ask and it will be given to you" (Mt. 7:7). We know the common teaching of the

---

1 Merit *de condigno* is based on justice, merit *de congruo* is based on *jure amicabili*, that is, on the rights of friendship.

theologians. True prayer, by which we ask with trusting humility and perseverance the graces necessary for our salvation, is infallibly efficacious (cf. S. T. II-II, q. 83, a. 15).

We know this doctrine; and yet, at times, it seems to us that we have truly prayed without being heard. We believe, or rather, we see the power of a machine, but we do not believe enough in the efficacy of prayer. From its results we see the power of that intellectual force that is science, and there is nothing very mysterious in it. In fact, we know where this force comes from, where it is directed and what human effects it produces. When we are dealing with prayer, however, we believe too weakly in its efficacy because we do not know whence it comes and we forget where it is directed. We ought to remember, then, what the source of the efficacy of prayer is and what the end is to which it tends, or rather, which it must attain.

The Source of the Efficacy of Prayer

The sources of rivers are found at high altitudes. The waters from the skies and the melting waters of snow and glaciers feed its course. In the beginning, before it fertilizes the valleys and goes on to rush into the sea, a river is a torrent that descends from the heights. This is a symbol of how highly exalted is the source of the efficacy of prayer.

Sometimes we erroneously believe that prayer is a force which has its first principle in us, and that prayer constitutes a means by which we are able to try to sway the will of God. Then our thoughts immediately strike against the following difficulty, often enunciated by unbelievers (in particular by the deists of the eighteenth and nineteenth centuries): no one is able to move the will of God, no one can change it. Without doubt God is the goodness that asks nothing other than to give itself, the mercy that is always ready to come to the aid of him who suffers. But God is also the perfectly immutable being, and His will is immutable. No one can boast of having illumined God, or of having changed His decrees. "I am the Lord and I do not change" (Mal. 3:6). Under the decrees of Providence the order of things and events is firmly and gently established from all eternity (cf. Num. 23:19, and Jas. 1:17).

Yes, all this is true. Yet, one should not, for this reason, fall into fatalism and conclude that prayer can do nothing and that what is to happen will happen according to fate, whether we pray or not. "Ask, and it will be given to you; search, and you will find; knock, and the door will be opened to you" (Mt. 7:7). This saying of the Gospel stands, and the interior life must search its meaning more and more. Thus, prayer is not a force that has its first principle in us; it is not an attempt of the human being to compel God to change His providential decrees. If sometimes we speak in this way, it is only by way of metaphor, and a human manner of expressing ourselves. In reality, the will of God is absolutely immutable. But it is precisely in this superior immutability that the source of the infallible efficacy of prayer is found.

Basically, it is the simplest thing. Despite the mystery of grace with which it is surrounded, we find here one of the most attractive and beautiful chiaroscuros. First of all, let us note what is clear. True prayer is infallibly efficacious because God, who cannot contradict Himself, has so decreed (S.T. II-II, q. 83, a. 2). The contemplation of the saints underlines all this.

The conception of a God who had not willed and foreseen from all eternity the prayers that we would direct to Him is just as childish as that of a God who would change His designs, disposing Himself according to our will. All has been foreseen (or at least permitted) from the beginning by a providential decree: not only what is to occur, but also the manner in which it is to happen and the causes that are to produce the events. For the material harvest the Lord has prepared the seed, the rain to help its germination and the sun to ripen the fruits of the earth. The same happens with the spiritual harvest. He has prepared the spiritual seed, the divine graces necessary for sanctification and salvation.

In each order, from the lowest to the most sublime, God prepares the causes that are to produce His determined effects. And prayer is one of these causes, destined to produce a particular effect, which is that of obtaining for us the gifts of God. All creatures exist solely by reason of the gifts of God, but the intellectual creature is the only one that can recognize this. Existence, health, physical strength, light of the intellect, moral energy, success in our undertakings, all these are gifts of God. But above all, grace, which leads us to our salvific good, makes us accomplish it and gives us the means to persevere, is a gift of God.

Grace—and even more the Holy Spirit, who has been sent to us and is the fountain of living water—is the preeminent gift of which Jesus spoke addressing the Samaritan woman: "If you only knew the gift of God, and Who it is Who says to you, 'Give Me to drink,' you, perhaps, would have asked of Him, and He would have given you living water, springing up unto life everlasting" (Jn. 4:10–14). The intellectual creature is the only one capable of realizing that it can live neither naturally nor supernaturally except through the gift of God. Why should we be surprised, then, if divine Providence has willed that man ask for graces? In this matter, as in all things, God wills the final effect first of all; then He disposes the means and causes that are to produce it. Having decided to give, He decides that we ought to pray in order to receive, just as a good father of a family, who has decided to give his children some pleasure, wants them to ask him for it.

Note that the gift of God is the result, while prayer is the means whereby it is obtained. St. Gregory the Great says that men must dispose themselves to receive what Almighty God has decided from eternity to give them. This is why Jesus, wishing to convert the Samaritan woman, disposes her to pray by saying to her: "If you knew the gift of God!" And just as He concedes to Magdalen an actual grace that is very strong yet very gentle, disposing her to repentance and prayer, so He acts in the same way with Zaccheus and the good thief.

Therefore, it is just as necessary to pray to gain the help of God which we need in order to do good and to persevere in it, as it is to sow in order to have grain. To those who say: "Whether we pray or whether we don't pray, what is to happen will happen," we must respond: "To speak in such a way is just as senseless as to say, 'Whether we sow or whether we don't sow with summer we shall have grain.'" Providence establishes not only the results but also the means we must use. It differs from fate inasmuch as it respects human liberty by giving grace as gentle as it is efficacious. Hence, an actual grace must be received in order to pray; but this is offered to all, and only he who voluntarily refuses it remains deprived of it.[2]

Therefore, prayer is necessary to obtain the help of God just as the seed is necessary for a harvest. Still there is this consid-

---

2 To every adult, even a great sinner, the efficacious grace to pray is offered. Every man receives from time to time the actual grace that renders prayer *really possible*. In this sufficient grace there is offered an efficacious help, just as in the blossom there is fruit. But if a man resists this so-called sufficient grace, he merits being deprived of efficacious grace which would enable him to pray effectively. Here is presented the mystery of resistance to grace, an evil deriving solely from our weakness; but the non-resistance, which is a good, comes primarily from God, the first source of every good. And since the love of God for us is the cause of every good, no one would be better than another if he were not loved more by God. "What do you have that you have not received?" (1 Cor. 4:7; cf. S.T. I, q. 20, a. 3 and 4). Our Lord has said, "Without me you can do nothing [in the order of salvation]" (Jn. 15:5). This is all the more reason to pray to him to grant us the grace, as he recommends to us. If, then, after having sincerely prayed with humility, confidence and perseverance, we did not obtain the helps necessary for our salvation, there would be a contradiction in God Himself and in his promises. These, however, are immutable and upon them the infallible efficacy of right prayer is based.

eration: the best seed, if lacking favorable external conditions, can remain unproductive—and thousands of seeds are lost in this way—yet humble and confident prayer, by which we ask for ourselves what is necessary for salvation, is never lost. We know that it is already heard by the very fact that it obtains for us the grace *to continue in prayer.*

This efficacy of properly said prayer is infallibly guaranteed us by Our Lord: "So I say to you: Ask, and it will be given to you; search, and you will find; knock, and the door will be opened to you. For the one who asks always receives; the one who searches always finds; the one who knocks will always have the door opened to him. What father among you would hand his son a stone when he asked for bread? Or hand him a snake instead of a fish? Or hand him a scorpion if he asked for an egg? If you then, who are evil, know how to give your children what is good, how much more will the Heavenly Father give the Holy Spirit to those who ask him?" (Lk. 11:9–13).

To His apostles He also said: "I tell you most solemnly, anything you ask for from the Father He will grant in My name. Until now you have not asked for anything in My name. Ask and you will receive, and so your joy will be complete" (Jn. 16:23–24).

The souls dedicated to prayer, even more than others, must live this doctrine which is elementary for every Christian. Hence, we must have confidence in the efficacy of prayer! This is not merely a human force that has its first principle in us; rather, the source of its efficacy is in God and in the infinite merits of the Savior. It descends from an eternal decree of love and reascends to divine mercy.

When we pray, it is certainly not a question of persuading God, of moving Him to change His providential dispositions; it is only a question of *lifting our will to His heights, to will with Him in time what He has decided to give us from eternity.* Prayer, far from tending to lower the Most High toward us, is rather an "elevation of the soul toward God," as the Fathers say. When we pray and are heard, it seems to us that the will of God has yielded toward us. It is our will, however, that is raised toward Him, in such a manner that we are disposed to will in time what God wills for us from eternity. From this follows that, far from being opposed to the divine directives, *prayer cooperates with them.* We are, therefore, two in willing, instead of one alone.

And when, for example, we have prayed much to obtain a conversion, and have been heard, we can rightly say that without doubt it is God who has converted this person, but He has deigned to associate me with Himself in this; from all eternity He had decided to have me pray to obtain this grace. Thus, we cooperate in our salvation by asking for the graces necessary to attain it. Among these graces there are some, like that of final perseverance, that cannot be merited[3] but are obtained by prayer that is humble, trusting and persevering.

Certainly, efficacious grace, which protects us from mortal sin and keeps us in the state of grace, cannot be merited, for it would be like meriting the very principle of merit (the continual state of grace). But, it can, be obtained by prayer. Thus, the actual and efficacious grace that is instrumental for a living contemplation, though it cannot, properly speaking, be merited *de condigno*, is obtained by prayer. "And so I prayed, and understanding was given me; I entreated, and the spirit of Wisdom came to me" (Wis. 7:7).

Also, when it is a question of our obtaining a grace of conversion for a person who may offer resistance, the more numerous we are who pray, each persevering in his prayer, the more we can hope to obtain this grace.

Hence, prayer cooperates powerfully in the plan of divine Providence. It can obtain anything whatsoever, on condition

---

3 The grace of final perseverance is, in fact, the state of grace that continues to death. It is to be noted, however, that the state of grace, being the principle of merit, cannot be merited (*cf. S.T.* I-II, q. 114, a. 9).

that we ask God first and foremost to love Him more and more: "Your Heavenly Father knows you need them all. Set your hearts on His Kingdom first, and on His righteousness, and all these other things will be given you as well" (Mt. 6:33).

If we do not obtain temporal goods, it means that they are not necessary for our salvation. But if our prayer is correctly made, we shall obtain in their place an even more precious grace for "the Lord is near to all who call upon Him, to all who call upon Him in truth" (Ps. 145:18). And the prayer of petition, if it is truly an elevation of the soul toward God, disposes us to a more intimate prayer of adoration, reparation, thanksgiving, and to the prayer of union.

CHAPTER XIII

Mental Prayer

> *I am the light of the world; anyone who follows Me will not be walking in the dark; he will have the light of life*—John 8:12
>
> *Still happier those who hear the word of God and keep it*—Luke 11:28

AFTER having considered the efficacy of prayer and its foundation, we now examine the essence of mental prayer, its various degrees, its object, what its preparation ought to be, and what its effects are.

What Is Mental Prayer?

The Fathers and all the masters of the spiritual life say that mental prayer is the elevation of the soul to God. Of this elevation it is easier to say what it is not, rather than what it is. To know what it is, it must be experienced. Indeed, we are not treating here simply of that elevation of soul required for all vocal prayers and absolutely necessary for all believers in order to be saved. "Mental prayer implies a much deeper consideration of the mysteries of faith. It is not indispensable for salvation, but surely very useful, and more or less indispensable with respect to the grade of perfection to which we are called" (Maynard I-12).

This mental prayer has always existed in the Church. Neither St. Teresa nor St. Ignatius introduced it. However, since in that era men no longer applied themselves spontaneously to mental prayer, it was necessary to make it obligatory and establish a determined time in the community for this purpose. Consequently different methods of mental prayer arose. As regards our Order, the duration of mental prayer was fixed by the General Chapter of 1515. But mental prayer itself had already been the practice for a long time.

The history of our Order recounts that a poor lay brother, who had become ill, did not recognize the priory of St. James when he returned because, as he said, he no longer saw the brethren in mental prayer before the altars. St. Thomas passed part of his nights in mental prayer. St. Albert composed a treatise on this subject. The life of our blessed father St. Dominic was a continuous mental prayer, day and night, whether in the priory or on the road.

From their foundation, the Carmelite and Cistercian Orders were dedicated to mental prayer. And what would characterize the interior life that was hidden in the catacombs in those souls ready for martyrdom during the first ages of the Church? How would we describe the life of Mary Magdalen after her conversion? and the life of St. John? of St. Paul and all the apostles? and the life of the Blessed Virgin? They were lives of contemplation and mental prayer.

Our Lord, who enjoyed the Beatific Vision, gave us an example when He felt the need of separating Himself from the apostles to retire into solitude. If He has recommended public prayer, He has also said: "And when you pray, do not imitate the hypocrites: they love to say their prayers standing up in the synagogues and at the street corners for people to see them. I tell you solemnly, they have had their reward. But when you pray, go to your private room and, when you have shut your door, pray to your Father who is in that secret place, and your Father who sees all that is done in secret will reward you" (Mt. 6:5–6).

Even before the coming of Our Lord, were there not individuals that knew interior prayer? Without it, how are we to understand the Psalms, the Book of Wisdom, the Canticle of Canticles? How can we believe that these divine books remained without being understood by all the people of the Old Testament? Mental prayer, then, implies a much deeper consideration of the mysteries of faith than vocal prayer. This consideration differs essentially from a simple study of the truth, from a philosophical or theological reflection.

It does not have ordinary knowledge as its end, but rather supernatural knowledge and love of the truth. Indeed, it is not only a question of an elevation of the intelligence, but of the elevation of the whole being toward God. It is a flight in which love contributes as much as intelligence. Actually love is the very principle and end of mental prayer.

"There are speculative souls," says Massoulié (*cf.* Maynard), "curious about the things of God, who are not, however, souls of mental prayer. If in their considerations they experience a pleasure that surpasses all the pleasures of the senses, this pleasure often derives solely from knowledge and not from charity. They are moved more by the love of knowledge than by the love of God, whom they wish to penetrate. Therefore, this pleasure often increases their pride and only serves to make them more filled with themselves."

St. Thomas made a distinction in his life between study and mental prayer. Although his studies proceeded from charity and were supernaturally fruitful, he felt the need of interrupting them, abandoning Aristotle and the tracts of the Fathers, to go and kneel before the altar and speak to God. Often he was taken unawares in tears during his prayer. If he had been only a scholar, he would not have been able to write the Office of the Most Blessed Sacrament as well as his commentaries on Aristotle. He himself, in his *Summa,* has clearly distinguished speculation from mental prayer or contemplation.

Speculation or study does not proceed necessarily from charity and does not terminate necessarily in the love of God: we can give ourselves to the study of theology without having charity. On the other hand, mental prayer or contemplation proceeds essentially from charity and terminates in an act of love of God.

It is through love that we seek to contemplate God, and the contemplation of the beauty and goodness of God increases our love. It is even necessary to say that here below contemplation is as a means to the end, in relation to love, since here below the love of God is more perfect than our knowledge of God. Indeed, love pushes us toward God, while knowledge of God draws God, in a certain way, into us and reduces Him, so to speak, to our proportions.

The goodness and beauty of God are infinitely superior to anything we can imagine. Thus, we can love Him more than we can know Him, and until we see Him face to face, love is more perfect than knowledge.

Finally, the purpose of contemplation here below is the act of love to which it leads. "*Terminus et finis vitae contemplativae habetur in affectu*"[1] *(S.T.* II-II, q. 180, a. 7 ad 1). Mental prayer has for its purpose the stirring up of the fire of charity. "In my thoughts, a fire blazed forth" (Ps. 39:4).

Acts of the three theological virtues and of the gift of wisdom. Mental prayer, in order to be the elevation of the whole person to God, must proceed from the three theological virtues: from faith, insofar as it is knowledge, and from hope and charity insofar as they are an act of love. But in mental prayer, or at least at the end of mental prayer, knowledge and love ought to blend in a certain

---

1   "The term also and the end of the contemplative life has its being in the appetite."

way into a single act. They should merge into a loving knowledge of God, into a look of love directed toward our Father who is in Heaven, toward His infinite perfections, toward Our Lord. This look of love in us proceeds from the most perfect of the gifts of the Holy Spirit, from the spirit of love that dwells in us, and from the gift of wisdom.

The Holy Spirit has us utter inexpressible moans and makes us cry out: "Abba, Father!"—the only word that children know to say to him who has given them life, who protects, instructs, and loves them. He allows us to consider something of divine truth (of the Most Holy Trinity, of the Incarnation, of the Redemption) by means of a taste, a touch, an intimate experience accompanied by the most absolute certainty. He reveals to us the hidden sense of the Gospel: "Taste and see that the Lord is sweet" (Ps. 34:9).

Under the impulse of the Holy Spirit, the will loves, with all its strength, the divine object which faith reveals to it. The intelligence judges experimentally something of the goodness of this object by means of the influence which the latter exercises on the will, which in turn, conforming itself to the object, becomes rectified. Even here below the dogmas of the Incarnation and Redemption fulfill and surpass our most legitimate and highest aspirations. By means of the dogmas, it is really God who makes Himself felt in us in the obscurity of our faith and is with us as a friend with a friend, no longer in purely speculative and abstract truths (as in a tract of theology), but as a living Person and source of life.

"Still happier those who hear the word of God and keep it!" says Our Lord to the poor woman who exclaims: "Happy the womb that bore You and the breasts You sucked!" (Lk. 11:28). If the Virgin is happy, it is not because she formed the body of the Savior but because she, in a certain way, first conceived Him in her spirit by means of prayer, and because she was united to Him by the most intimate knowledge and most ardent love.

This mental prayer, this gaze of love, is the repose of the person in God, a repose that presupposes the hard work of mortification and crowns it. As St. Cyril of Alexandria said, "It is the respite of the soul immersed in the beauty of God through contemplation, experiencing His love by means of charity."

The Various Degrees

In mental prayer we have as many degrees as there are in the gift of wisdom, which increases with the growth of charity. Some simple persons without instruction, and the Christian virgins in particular, often have the gift of wisdom in a much more exalted way than theologians.

We can distinguish three degrees. In the first degree of mental prayer are found those who have begun the spiritual life and feel a repugnance for evil and attraction for good. In the second are those who are making progress through renunciation and mortification. In the third are those who are perfectly emptied of themselves, whose purified virtues reach heroism.

"Generally, the perfect are called to a contemplation that is neither acquired nor maintained except by the assiduous exercise of meditation and in consequence of a passive contemplation that does not depend on human activity but only on divine goodness, which of itself works in us" (Maynard II-10). St. Teresa (*Way of Perfection,* chap. 19) distinguishes these two contemplations by comparing the passive prayer to a fountain of spring water and the active prayer to water that has already run for some time on the ground and has lost its clearness, mixing itself with the mud that is carried along. In fact, in passive prayer the fountain of spring water is the Holy Spirit, who offers Himself immediately to us, works in us and separates us from the world with the knowledge He gives us. On the other hand, in active contemplation, which is the fruit of our meditation, there is the imperfection of our human acts mixed like mud in the water of grace and divine truth. Thus, when we rouse ourselves to a contempt of the world, this consideration, since it still remains human, fastens our thoughts on objects which basically still please us (St. Teresa, *ibid.*).

Nothing like this remains in passive prayer. God snatches us from the world, draws us to Himself and, in an instant, gives us a vision of all things here below that is much clearer than we could acquire by many years of assiduous meditation (St. Teresa, *ibid.; cf.* also Catherine of Siena, *Dial.* chap. 100). In reality, in this state the mastery of the gifts of the Holy Spirit over the virtues and over the human way of acting is realized: it represents the adult stage of the spiritual life.

But in this living spring water there are so many different levels! (Maynard, II, pp. 192–256). They vary from that of a soul who attains passive prayer for himself alone, to those souls overflowing with divine life, as a St. Dominic, who attain it for a whole religious order, and finally to that unique soul, the Holy Virgin, who sustains all of us by her prayer.

These eminent degrees of the gift of wisdom and of loving knowledge are entirely independent of any visions, supernatural words or revelations, which do not presuppose the state of grace as being necessary and which are not themselves necessary to the full development of charity, but are given, rather, as with the grace of miracles, to cooperate in the sanctification and salvation of other souls.

The Object

What is the object of mental prayer? In the first place, it is obviously the One and Triune God and all that revelation makes known of His nature and infinite perfections. Then, in a particular way, it is Our Lord Jesus Christ, who is the indispensable way for all to be lifted up to God, even for those who are already much advanced in the spiritual life. Further, it is His Passion and Death on the Cross, contemplated in the light of the divine attributes of justice and mercy which illumine Our Lord's sacrifice. We especially cite the spectacle of the Cross, which nourishes charity, since this is the greatest proof of love that God has given us: "God loved the world so much that He gave His only Son" (Jn. 3:16). Since no one goes to the Father except through the Son, without Our Lord one may have a philosophic, abstract knowledge but not that supernatural, experimental, affective knowledge which is the heart of mental prayer.

A secondary object of mental prayer is creatures, insofar as they manifest God to us. Among all the creatures we refer to those in which the image of God appears more clearly: the souls of the saints and the Mystical Body of Christ.

Another object of mental prayer is our life, which ought to be guided by the will of God to produce in us the image of our divine model, Jesus Christ. He is the image, the splendor of the Father and the manifestation of His nature (*cf.* Heb. 1:3).

We have examined mental prayer, its principle, end, degrees, and object. Now we will consider its practice.

How to Go about Mental Prayer

Venerable Louis of Granada says that many believe that mental prayer is like any art; hence, to be perfect, it is enough to learn its method and apply it mechanically. Their illusion derives from the fact that certain modern authors, after setting down a method of mental prayer, lead us to believe that these rules, if observed conscientiously, can take the place of divine grace. This, however, is a very naturalistic concept of mental prayer. Without doubt the methods of mental prayer are useful and often necessary, especially for beginners; but mental prayer depends essentially on the grace of God and the action of the Holy Spirit. It is the Holy Spirit's word that we hear in ourselves and which we prepare ourselves to receive primarily by practicing humility and conforming to the will of God.

Others fall into the opposite excess. They disregard all methods and all preparation and then they complain that, when they wish to recollect themselves and put themselves in the presence of God, they find nothing except emptiness and darkness.

Remote preparation. Mental prayer presupposes a remote preparation and a proximate preparation. Remote preparation is none other than mortification of our passions and the detachment from the world and from ourselves through humility. It is clear that if our spirit is preoccupied with pleasures and affairs of the world, if our soul is agitated by passions, by affections that are too human, or by jealousy, we are not disposed to mental prayer. If we are habitually preoccupied with ourselves, if we ignore humility, how can we let ourselves be penetrated by God and hear His voice? Without mortification and humility the methods of mental prayer are worthless.

The best remote preparation is the diligent practice of the three vows—which detach the soul from pleasures, from the things of the world and from self—together with patience in bearing the crosses that mortify us. If you are faithful today in avoiding venial sin, gossip and vain conversations, tomorrow God will also be faithful and will let you hear His word in mental prayer.

Proximate preparation. Proximate preparation must dispose the intelligence and will. It is necessary to dispose our intellect with the selection of a determined subject. "He who wishes for too much, attains nothing." Unless our attention is fixed on something precise, we run the risk of not thinking of anything.

It would be preferable to choose a subject from the life of Our Lord since He is the Way, the Truth, and the Life. He is the expression and beauty of God which has been given us. He is our model for as long as we are wayfarers on this earth. In Him is epitomized the sum total of faith, dogma, and morals. St. Teresa counsels us to meditate on the life of Jesus according to the cycle of the liturgical year, uniting our prayer to that of the universal Church and that of Our Lord, who does not cease interceding for His Church. Let us not meditate on the joy of the Epiphany on Good Friday! Finally, when we consider the life of Our Lord we should take time to meditate preferably on the virtues that are opposed to our predominant fault, those we put in practice less than the others. Above all we should learn from Him to be meek and humble of heart, precisely as He Himself has taught us.

Once the subject has been chosen, it is necessary to prepare our will by prayer. For mental prayer it is not enough, as we have said, to speculate; it is also necessary to love, to make our will conform to the divine will. Only prayer can obtain for us this grace of conformity, thus placing us in the presence of God.

After having prayed, we must meditate on the chosen subject. Whether it is a virtue of Our Lord or a fact from His life, we must follow in our meditation the order indicated to us in the Our Father. This means that we think first of God and then of ourselves. We contemplate the glory of God in the virtues of the divine Master, the Kingdom of God they procure, and the fulfillment of the will of God.

We might pause a moment in our mental prayer at the climactic point of the Our Father to let our intelligence give to the will the time to love, to savor God in Our Lord, to take joy in His glory. We should listen to Him if He wishes to speak to us—if we have merited that He speak to us. We should remain thus as long as our love is awake, and then, let us descend to ask for our daily bread and the strength to put into practice the example that we have meditated on, as well as the strength to resist temptation. We should pardon others and ask pardon for the past. Then, we ought to make a resolution for the future, not a vague one, however, that would remain inefficacious, but a precise one, based on the meditated subject as it relates to our life.

If meditation according to this manner, though very simple, is nonetheless not possible to us, if we are not able to repulse distractions or recollect ourselves sufficiently to meditate, or if we find only aridity and desolation, we should undertake prayer of the heart. This consists simply in willing to remain in the presence of God in order to love Him more than ourselves, in abandoning ourselves to the divine will, in being happy in our nothingness and acknowledging that God is infinitely above all that we can possibly imagine.

This affective mental prayer is one of the most fruitful if the soul is humble and generous. It is distinguished from lazy inertia by the vigilance of love—this remains the essential act of mental prayer. In a certain sense, this prayer is easier than the other forms because not all souls are capable of remaining in profound reasoning, but almost all can easily produce affective movements while meditating on the Our Father and the manner in which they put it into practice in their lives. Every Christian is capable of reentering thus into himself if he mortifies and denies himself.

The Effects

Now we shall speak of the effects of mental prayer. The impetratory effect of prayer is, as we know, to obtain infallibly the grace necessary to salvation when we ask for it with humility, trust and perseverance. If God did not listen to this true prayer He would be contradicting Himself, for He commands us to save ourselves, admonishes us that grace is indispensable to be saved, and tells us to pray to obtain this grace. Hence, if He did not listen to true prayer, which He Himself inspires and commands, He would no longer be God.

Mental prayer, however, does not have only an impetratory effect. It develops in us all the virtues, and especially the three virtues which together with humility are the heart of the Christian life: faith, hope, and charity. We should give ourselves courageously, then, to mental prayer so that our faith may not be simply that superficial and verbal knowledge that stops at formulas, but rather that which penetrates the intimate sense of the divine word. We should give ourselves to mental prayer so that we may learn to hope in God alone, instead of trusting in ourselves and counting on others. We ought to give ourselves to mental prayer so that we may love God with the love He wants, with the love He showed us on the Cross and continues to show us in the Eucharist.

We should give ourselves to mental prayer so that we may extend our love for God to all the souls loved by God, to those who make us suffer as well as those who please us. We should pray for all souls—that will be an apostolate more fruitful than a sermon without love. We ought to pray, like St. Catherine of Siena, in the name of Our Lord and of all the souls that make up His Mystical Body. Like her, we should take up in our soul all these souls and place them in the heart of God. We ought, like her, to make catholic acts, that is, universal acts of contrition, of faith, hope, and charity. In this way our mental prayer will lose itself in the prayer of Christ Himself, always living; and He will carry us to God on the wings of the Spirit of Love.

Perseverance in Mental Prayer

> *If you only knew what God is offering. . .*
> *you would have been the one to ask, and*
> *He would have given you living water—*
> *John 4:10*
>
> *If any man is thirsty, let him come to Me!*
> *Let the man come and drink who believes*
> *in Me! As Scripture says: From his breast*
> *shall flow fountains of living water—*
> *John 7:37–38*

WE have said that mental prayer is the elevation of the whole being to God. In it knowledge and love must be merged into a gaze of love that is none other than the contemplation of God and of Our Savior and model, Jesus Christ. We have also considered how we ought to prepare ourselves for mental prayer and how, if it is impossible to apply ourselves to that which is properly called meditation, we ought to replace it with prayer of the heart.

Necessity of This Perseverance

Now we must speak of perseverance in mental prayer. St. Teresa tells us in fact that in mental prayer perseverance is the trait most necessary *(Interior Castle,* II Mansion, chap. I). With it we cannot help but gain much; without it we can lose all. We must engage in battle against ourselves, against our spiritual sloth and against the Devil who wants to throw us into discouragement. How many souls, deprived of the sweetness they tasted at the beginning, have turned back after having put their hand to the plow! What is more, some souls that were very advanced have fallen backwards.

St. Catherine of Genoa, who from the age of thirteen had given herself to mental prayer and had made great progress, became discouraged after five years of suffering. She abandoned the interior life and for five years led the life of a worldly woman. But one day she observed with anguish the frightful emptiness of her soul and felt the desire that a holy life be reborn in her. Without warning, God had called her to Himself, striking her as He did St. Paul on the way to Damascus. After fourteen years of terrible penance that is almost beyond description, she received the certainty of having fully satisfied divine justice. She used to say: "If I were to turn back, I would wish that my eyes be plucked out, and I would find that this would still not suffice" (Hello, *Physiognomy of the Saints*).

Other souls that have fought the battle a long time, become discouraged when they are at last only a few steps from the fountain of living water, and they fall back again. Without mental prayer they no longer have the strength to bear their cross, and therefore they return to an easy and superficial life. Others could be saved in this lax existence but these souls run the great risk of being lost because their faculties, which are extremely powerful, will push them to excesses. Excess was permitted and demanded of them when it was a question of the love of God, but every other excess will drag them into the abyss. Souls made for great things carry within themselves a grave risk. Since a mediocre life is not possible for them, they take sides without any half-measures—with God or against God.

Thus it is that the angels can know only ardent charity or irremissible mortal sin—venial sin is impossible for them. They see perfectly and bind themselves totally in all their acts. Angels or Devils, the holiest or the worst, these are the only alternatives for pure spirits. It is, therefore, a great danger for a soul that has once given itself to mental prayer not to persevere in it, or to participate in it only in a material way and without any drive of love. The abandonment of the life of mental prayer can be the beginning of its ruin.

To persevere in mental prayer it is necessary, first, to trust in the Lord, who calls all souls to the fountain of living water and hence offers them the grace to overcome their obstacles. Secondly, we must allow ourselves to be led humbly through the way He has chosen for us, conforming our will fully to His.

To Trust

First of all we must trust in the Lord. To fall backwards in the face of difficulties, such as distraction or aridity, and thus become discouraged means both to lack in the virtue of hope recommended to us by the Lord and also to doubt in the goodness and power of God. Some souls, to excuse their discouragement, their laziness and their cowardice, will say: "One must not fall into presumption. Mental prayer was made only for some souls, not for me. God is not calling me to that height; it would be presumption to pretend that He is." Thus, with the pretext of avoiding presumption we are lacking in hope and put the responsibility for our spiritual inertia on God.

To combat discouragement and to stir up hope within ourselves, we should seek to understand thoroughly this truth that is insufficiently stressed: God calls all souls to the fountain of living water of mental prayer after a period of time, more or less long and after trials that can be more or less painful. When I speak of living water, I do not mean visions or revelations.

I am speaking of that affective gaze of love that enables the soul to quench its thirst at the very fountain of life which is the Holy Spirit present in us. I am referring to that elevated degree of the gift of wisdom through which God works in us without our human activity, to make Himself felt by us. The word of God that is tasted through the diligent effort of meditation and through our own human activity, is, on the other hand, like water mixed with mud.

The greater number of past authors on spirituality, especially those of the Dominican School basing themselves on the authority of St. Thomas, maintain that all souls are called to this living water. (Maynard II, N. 75; Arintero, *Mystical Evolution,* pp. 447–510). They are called to the fountain of mental prayer, if not to pour it out over a great number of souls as did the saints, then at least to the extent required to attain what is necessary for the perfection of their own personal charity. To establish this truth we must bring out the testimony of Sacred Scripture, especially the words of Our Lord, and find the precise meaning in the light of sound theological conclusions.

The testimony of Sacred Scripture is very clear. Already in the Old Testament the Book of Wisdom invites all souls without distinction: "Look forward, therefore, to my words; yearn for them, and they will instruct you. Wisdom is bright, and does not grow dim. By those who love her she is readily seen, and found by those who look for her. Quick to anticipate those who desire her, she makes herself known to them. Watch for her early and you will have no trouble. . . .I reckoned no priceless stone to be her peer, for compared with her, all gold is a pinch of sand, and beside her silver ranks as mud. . . .In her company all good things came to me!" (Wis. 6:11–14; 7:9–11). The same invitation is found in Psalm 34: "Taste and see how sweet the Lord is," and in Proverbs (8:17 and 35): "I love those who love me; those who seek me eagerly shall find me. . .for the man who finds me finds life, he will win favor from Yahweh." In Isaiah it is predicted that "Your sons will all be taught by Yahweh. The prosperity of your sons will be great" (Isa. 54:13).

Our Lord explains these words of the Old Testament. He compares Himself to the good shepherd (Jn. 10:1) who leads his sheep to pasture, calling each one by name. They follow him because they hear his voice and recognize it. In the same way Our Lord leads our souls to the eternal pastures, that we may be nourished not only by bread, but by the word of God, by the mystery of the Kingdom of Heaven. At the center of these eternal pastures is found the fountain of living water about which Jesus spoke to the sinful Samaritan woman in spite of her mistakes. "If you only knew what God is offering and who it is that is saying to you: Give Me a drink, you would have been the one to ask, and He would have given you living water" (Jn. 4:10).

At Jerusalem on one of the great feast days, Jesus stood at the foot of the temple and cried out to all, not just to some privileged ones: "If any man is thirsty, let him come to Me! Let the man come and drink who believes in Me! As Scripture says (Isa. 58:11): From his breast shall flow fountains of living water" (Jn. 7:37–38).

This fountain of living water *(fons vivus)*—as Our Lord will later explain—is the Holy Spirit, the Counselor whom He sends, who teaches all things and enables us to penetrate the intimate sense of the Gospel. This Holy Spirit, the principle of the seven gifts, dwells in us through charity, as St. Paul says. Consequently, the Holy Spirit is found in every soul that is in the state of grace. Certainly it is not in order to remain inactive that the Spirit dwells there. It is not to be silent that the Divine Counselor lives in us. On the contrary, the Holy Spirit does not cease to speak to souls, as the author of the *Imitation* (III, chap. 3) says, but many are deaf to His voice because they are listening to the voice of the world or to themselves. The Holy Spirit is in the soul and operates there in proportion to the growth of charity. And He says, not only to privileged souls but to all: "Love the Lord your God with your whole heart, and with your whole soul, and with your whole mind, and with your whole strength" (*cf.* Deut. 6:5; Mk. 12:30). Do not set limits for your love!

Evidently, then, according to the testimony of the Lord, all souls are called to nourish themselves in the eternal pastures, to quench their thirst at the fountain of the living water of mental prayer and to be interiorly instructed by the Spirit of God. It is our fault if there are "many called and few chosen." The fault lies in our lack of humility and love. If we were more humble and more devoutly intent on having the Kingdom of God in us, then wisdom, which hides itself from the prudent and the wise, would be revealed to us and no one could accuse us of presumption.

Theology makes the teachings in Sacred Scripture still more precise (*cf. S.T.* I-II, q. 68, a. 1 and 2). St. Thomas explains that with regard to Heaven, our supernatural end, the moral virtues are not sufficient; nor are the theological virtues of faith, hope, and charity. They are insufficient because they still operate in a human mode, submitting themselves to the manner of acting of our human faculties, which is restricted and limited like the human being himself.[1] So it is that faith reveals God to us in a manner that is too abstract, too obscure, and in formulas that are too narrow. So it is that the initiatives of hope and charity, as long as they are tempered by prudence—even though it is Christian prudence—do not go beyond a certain measure, a happy medium that still remains human.

---

1 Through the theological and moral virtues man is not perfected in the order related to his ultimate end in such a way that he no longer needs to be moved by a certain superior inspiration of the Holy Spirit (*S.T.* I-II, q. 68, a. 2 ad 2).

This mixture of the divine and the human in the supernatural virtues leaves us in a state of inferiority. Hence, through them we are not sufficiently equipped to attain our supernatural end. We must, in fact, attain it not only by supernatural acts, but by supernatural acts performed supernaturally—by an impetus that can come only from God. St. Thomas says that by the virtues alone we find ourselves before our supernatural end like beginners left to themselves. The beginner, who still does not know his trade well, knows what is to be done but does not know how to do it as it should be done. For this reason it is necessary that the master who is training him take hold of his hand and himself guide the work so that it may be presentable.

Thus our mental prayer remains too human to truly taste the word of God. As long as it remains only the fruit of diligent meditation, we, as St. Teresa says, drink only a water mixed with mud that runs along the ground; this is the human mode of our activity *(Way of Perfection,* chap. 19). To drink at the fountain of living water, it is necessary that the Holy Spirit directly intervene, take possession of our intelligence and will and communicate to them His divine manner of thinking and loving. "With our mouth He utters inexpressible sounds." Only this divine manner of acting is worthy of God, who must be known not as an abstract truth but as a living truth. He must be infinitely loved.

As long as we remain here below, we will always be beginners. Therefore, if we wish our mental prayer and our works to be perfect it is necessary that the Holy Spirit intervene habitually. And consequently it is necessary to admit, besides the virtues, the permanent action of the gifts of the Holy Spirit which make us docile to His action, to His inspirations, and to His direction. The first of these gifts is that of wisdom.

With only the ordinary exercise of the gifts of the Holy Spirit we can attain even now the adult stage of the supernatural life and become good disciples of the Holy Spirit, habitually docile to the voice of the Master, always ready to hear His voice. St. Paul says: "Everyone moved by the Spirit is a son of God. . . . And if we are children we are heirs as well" (Rom. 8:14 and 17). In the Psalms it is written: "May your good Spirit guide me on the right way in the land of the saints" (Ps. 143:10). This means, St. Thomas concludes, that no one can obtain this celestial inheritance unless he is moved and led by the Holy Spirit.

If we observe that the gift of wisdom increases with charity and that charity increases with humility, denial of self, and conformity to the will of God, then we must necessarily conclude that, since all men are called to grow in charity, they are consequently called to grow in wisdom to the extent of surpassing their human manner of thinking. This is exactly what Our Lord calls "drinking at the fountain of living water." For this reason, after having said, "If anyone wants to be a follower of Mine, let him renounce himself and take up his cross and follow Me" (Mt. 16:24), He adds, "Anyone who follows Me will not be walking in the dark; he will have the light of life" (Jn. 8:12).

Therefore, all men are called to this light of life after the necessary purifications, which can be more or less painful, more or less lengthy, according to their imperfections and according to the degree of divine life to which God predestines them. He submits to longer trials those He wishes to bring to a greater height, but He calls all, after the necessary purifications, to taste His word of life.

The dogma of Purgatory, also, confirms this conclusion when it teaches us that there are certain purifications absolutely indispensable for all souls before they can enter Heaven. Hence, if one does not undergo these purifications with merit in this life, he necessarily undergoes them in the next, but without merit or progress in charity. Consequently, there is no presumption in desiring this living water of mental prayer, just as there is none in desiring daily Communion, although the Jansenists said the contrary. Our Lord does not cease to call the little ones and to thank His Father for having revealed to them what He hides from the prudent and the wise. If we truly desire it, the sense of the divine certainly will be given us.

It would be presumption, however, to desire the living water immediately, without going through the intermediate stages, without the will to become more detached from the world and from self, without the will to become more humble, without the will to pledge oneself totally to conformity with God's will. It would be the kind of presumption one might commit in receiving Holy Communion daily without desiring to correct oneself. That would be falling into what St. John of the Cross calls "spiritual greed": seeking spiritual consolations for themselves and not for God. It is not the consolation which we should seek and love, but God, who gives the consolation to those who truly love Him for Himself.

It would be presumption to desire the more exalted degrees God reserves for the saints, who, like St. Dominic, are predestined to exercise a great influence on His Mystical Body. Like the publican of the Gospel (Lk. 18:13) and all the saints, we ought to stand in the last place, conform our will in all things to that of God, desire His Kingdom and think of Him. Then, it will be He who thinks of us and makes us grow continually to the degree to which He has decided to lead us.

It would be presumption to desire and to ask for visions and revelations rather than the living water, that is, the light of life and the intimate sense of the words of our divine Master. Visions and revelations are extraordinary favors which do not necessarily suppose the state of grace and are not at all needed for a superior development of charity. Like miracles, they have a utility that is rather external (that is, for one's neighbor) and if they are not accompanied by a profound humility, they can also become dangerous, not in themselves, but incidentally. The danger arises inasmuch as they may make their recipients become complacent with themselves and may lead them to illusions (*cf.* Arintero). But to ask for the meaning of the divine is not a presumption. On the contrary, it is necessary to desire it with ardor. "Ask and it shall be given you, seek and you shall find, knock and it shall be opened to you."

We should conclude then, that we must never become discouraged before difficulties that we meet in mental prayer, be they distractions or aridity. Our Lord, who calls us to the goal, also offers us the graces necessary to triumph over these obstacles. We must, however, look to see whether these difficulties come from our lukewarmness or are a trial sent by the Lord to purify us. "They come from our lukewarmness," says St. John of the Cross, "if, not having a taste for the things of God, we instead have a taste for the things of the world; and if we do not have a true desire of serving God and making progress in perfection. On the contrary, if we are detached from the world and truly desirous of serving God in a perfect way, these difficulties are a trial willed by God."

If the obstacles come from our lukewarmness, it is a sign that the deficiency lies in our remote preparation for mental prayer. In that case we must give ourselves generously to a more perfect practice of mortification, of humility, and of the three vows. If it is a question of a trial, however, we must wait patiently and with loving resignation. If meditation is impossible for us, we should undertake the prayer of conformity to the will of God which consists in willing to remain in that state, to serve Him and to acknowledge that He is infinitely above all that we could possibly meditate. We should not lose courage. That hour is not lost because, despite the impotence of our thought, love was awakened and this is what is essential.

To Allow Oneself to Be Led

We must also allow ourselves to be led through the way that the Lord has chosen for us. To attain the living waters it is not enough to hope in Our Lord; we must also allow ourselves to be led with docility through the way He has outlined for us. There is a great way, common to all souls without exception: humility and conformity to the will of God. All ought to pray like the publican and hold themselves in the last place. It has been said for all that God exalts the humble and humbles the proud; the mysteries of God, hidden from the wise and the prudent, are revealed to the little ones.

This is the only way that leads to the living waters. Yet, along this way there are some rocky places where it is difficult to walk, while in other places it is smoother and covered with new grass; one part of the road is scorched by the sun, while the other part is shady.

The Good Shepherd leads His sheep as He thinks best. He leaves some souls in the difficult passes for a long time to make them stronger because He has the intention of leading them to a greater height. St. Teresa remained fourteen years unable to meditate except by reading; even this was wearisome for her. During his apostolic voyages, Bl. Diego of Cadiz, although he exerted a profound influence on souls, did not find anything except dryness, confusion, and filial fear in his daily three hours of mental prayer; only very rarely did he feel and taste the sweetness of the divine charity which burned in him.

If Our Lord raises the Marys instead of the Marthas to contemplation, He also reserves for them, in the midst of their contemplation, some crosses that are much more painful. Without suffering as much, the Marthas, too, attain the living waters; even if they do not attain them with as much abundance, nonetheless, they quench their thirst and are satiated in proportion to their desire.

There are some individuals that arrive at contemplation very late, says St. Teresa, and sometimes they can pray only vocally. Yet, a truly humble person ought to be content with the road along which Our Lord leads it; it then enjoys divine wisdom and the light of life, even if not always fully conscious of it.

We cannot better condense this doctrine, nor better penetrate it and convince ourselves that it is truly the traditional doctrine of the whole Church than by reading *The Imitation of Christ* (III, chap. 3), on the necessity of listening to the word of God with humility, and by reading the following prayer to implore the grace of devotion: "Speak, O Lord, because your servant listens. You alone have the words of eternal life; make them descend like dew so that my soul may not become like earth without water."

CHAPTER XV

Docility to the Holy Spirit

The Lord Yahweh has opened my ear. For
my part, I made no resistance, neither did
I turn away—Isaiah 50:5

WE have said that, if we persevere in mental prayer, we shall
finally hear the voice of the Holy Spirit, who gives us the sense
of divine things and prompts us on to works of salvation. At
this point, we will consider docility to the Holy Spirit and the
means that can enable us to distinguish His voice from those
which could lead us into error.

The Movement of the Spirit

Docility to the Holy Spirit is necessary for the salvation of
every Christian soul: "Everyone moved by the Spirit is a son of
God" (Rom 8:14), and "Your good Spirit will guide me on level
ground" (Ps. 143:10). Without the movement and direction of
the Holy Spirit we cannot arrive at this goal; the supernatural
virtues, even if guided by Christian prudence, are insufficient.
This prudence, however supernatural it may be, still retains a
human mode that is too timid to walk befittingly in the ways
of Our Lord. We must hasten toward divine things in a divine
manner, not in a human way. Only the Holy Spirit, by His
movement and immediate direction can give us this divine
impetus. Since we are beginners, the Holy Spirit must take

possession of our intelligence and our will in order that we may accomplish the divine works in a divine manner.

Our Lord said to us: "I shall ask the Father, and He will give you another Advocate to be with you forever, that Spirit of truth whom the world can never receive since it neither sees nor knows Him; but you know Him, because He is with you, He is in you. I will not leave you orphans" (Jn. 14:16–18).

The divine Spirit, whom the Apostles received at Pentecost and whom all Christians receive through confirmation, is the soul of the Church, the soul of the Mystical Body of which Christ is the head. The head cannot communicate an influx to the members by way of the nerves if it and the members are not animated by the same spirit. There is only one soul for the whole body; it is whole in the entire body and whole in every part, though it is more eminently in the head since it is there that it exercises its most elevated operations.

The same occurs in the Mystical Body. The head is the soul of Christ, the members are the souls in the state of grace, and the vital influx is constituted by the actual graces, the inspirations and attractions that move us to accomplish the good. The one soul of this whole spiritual body is the Holy Spirit, and, just as our will directs our head and by means of it the other members of our body, so the Holy Spirit moves the soul of Christ and by means of it our souls.

During sleep our head and members live their respective lives without the intervention of our will; but when we are awake the matter is quite different. Thus it is that, as long as our supernatural life is still drowsy and unconscious, we act in a human mode, according to our human way of being. But when it becomes more conscious, more active, and we feel a kind of divine impetus, it is the Holy Spirit, the Spirit of Christ, moving us by means of His gifts.

Some authors say that the action of the gifts of the Holy Spirit is reserved solely to the practice of heroic virtues, and that in the practice of the ordinary virtues these gifts remain inactive. Instead, many others, especially among the Thomists, think that even though the influence of these gifts is predominant in the heroic virtues, it extends, nevertheless, to an infinite number of practical cases in daily Christian life. They cite, for example, when there is need for a greater readiness to tame the passions and to resist the temptations of the Devil and the world, especially, when the infirmity and weakness of the subject requires a more complete and efficacious help, a principle of action more elevated than the ordinary virtue.

All persons, therefore, ought to show themselves docile to the action of the Holy Spirit within them; all those in the state of grace have the gifts of the Holy Spirit, and these gifts are not in them to remain inactive. We must be docile to the Holy Spirit by practicing all the virtues. He is our master for contemplation and action, in all the events and circumstances of our life. Faith, hope and charity are rendered more active, particularly through the gifts of understanding, knowledge, and wisdom. Prudence is animated by the gift of counsel; justice and religion by the gift of piety; fortitude by the gift of the same name; and temperance by the gift of fear of the Lord. The gift of fear of the Lord helps in the fight against the attraction of prohibited pleasures and inspires the mortifications of a St. Louis Bertrand and a St. Rose of Lima, and the preaching of a St. Vincent Ferrer.

The gift of fortitude reanimates our courage in time of danger, sustaining St. Peter Martyr in his office and John of Gorcum in his torment; giving strength to St. Catherine de Ricci when she was commanded to spit on her vision, and enabling her to bear heroically the prejudices of the community against her.

The gift of piety makes us better able to understand and practice our religious duties and it inspires us with an affection for God that is wholly filial. This gift is revealed to us especially in the life of a St. Agnes of Montepulciano or a St. Pius V.

The gift of counsel directs us in the particularly difficult circumstances of life and surpasses our prudence. It was in this gift that St. Antoninus, Archbishop of Florence, excelled.

The gift of knowledge enables us to judge correctly human things when they are opposed to the divine; it shows us their vanity. It makes us feel, above all, the infinite gravity of sin as an offense to God and a damage to the soul. It is this gift of knowledge which made St. Dominic cry when he exclaimed during his prayers: "Lord, Lord, why are there sinners?" The profound thought of moral miseries caused the saint a deep sadness that often made him weep in the pulpit.

The gift of understanding enables us to comprehend the truths of faith and grasp their meaning hidden under the letter; it penetrates beyond appearances and makes the hidden thought burst out. It is the gift of understanding that illumines the words of Sacred Scripture in the *Dialogues* and *Letters* of St. Catherine of Siena.

Finally, the gift of wisdom infuses us with such a sense of God and divine things that it enables us to judge all things in relation to their first cause and their ultimate end. It was the gift of wisdom that presided at the composition of that wonderful synthesis, the *Summa* of St. Thomas. In it all, absolutely all, is subordinated to the idea of God, the point of meeting for every judgment regarding man, human liberty, and social life. Whatever subject St. Thomas treats, fundamentally it is always of God that he speaks because he connects everything to its first cause and its ultimate reason for existence. And it was the gift of wisdom that also nourished his mental prayer and dictated to him the office of the feast of Corpus Christi.

These seven gifts, these seven divine inspirations, are present in us—even if not in the same measure as they are found in the

great saints—and it is the same supernatural quality of light and
love that should inspire our life. Hence, we should be docile to
this inspiration, to that voice of the Spirit, in mental prayer, in
work, in the common life, and in the midst of difficulties that
we meet.

That Voice

To be docile to the voice of the Holy Spirit we must be able
to hear it and learn to distinguish it from all others that could
draw us into error. *To be able to hear it,* it is necessary that we be
recollected, detached from the world, and practice mortification
of our heart, of our will, and of our judgment. If there is no
silence in our soul and the voice of the world and the passions
agitate it, we cannot hear the interior word of our Master. If we
habitually take pleasure in our own way of seeing things and do
not wish to receive counseling from anyone, we shall hear, above
all else, ourselves, or else a perfidious and dangerous voice that
seeks the way of our heart.

To hear the voice of the Holy Spirit, then, it is necessary that
we obtain silence within ourselves by interior mortification and
detachment. Even then this voice of the Spirit remains mysterious, as Our Lord said to Nicodemus: "The wind blows wherever
it pleases; you hear its sound, but you cannot tell where it comes
from or where it is going. That is how it is with all who are born
of the Spirit" (Jn. 3:8).[1] In fact, this voice begins as an inspiration, as an obscure light; but if one perseveres in humility and
conformity to the will of God, it clearly shows its divine origin
to the conscience and, though it remains mysterious, it becomes

---

1 Hello, in regard to St. Catherine of Genoa, says: "In the life of the saints,
and especially in the life of the contemplative saints, there is a succession
of incomprehensible steps: they hesitate, they vacillate, they move ahead,
they turn back, they change their paths. One has the impression that they are
wasting time. It seems that the mysterious ways through which they are led
never finish. God teaches them humility and makes them understand their
impotence and nothingness" (Hello, *Physiognomy of the Saints*, p. 310).

the shining night that Sacred Scripture speaks of: "And night is my illumination in my delights" (Ps. 139:12).

To avoid all illusions we must *learn to distinguish* the Spirit of God from two other spirits or inspirations which at the beginning seem right, but lead to death. St. John says: "It is not every spirit, my dear people, that you can trust; test them" (1 Jn. 4:1). Besides the Spirit of God, there is also the spirit of the Devil, who sometimes transforms himself into an angel of light. There is also the purely natural spirit that proceeds from our fallen human nature, which, with its drives and enthusiasms, is a source of illusion.

As a rule, it is one of these three spirits that dominates in a soul: in perverse souls it is the spirit of the Devil, in lukewarm souls the natural spirit. In those that have begun to give themselves to the interior life, however, the Spirit of God habitually dominates, although there is still much interference from the natural spirit and the spirit of evil. Even in perfect souls God permits certain imperfections—sometimes more apparent than real—to maintain them in humility and give them the occasion to practice the opposite virtues.

It is, therefore, important both to distinguish well which is the spirit that prompts us to act, and also to understand in what things we are "of God," as St. John says, and in what things we are "of ourselves." To distinguish which spirit is making us act, we must discern the results of its influence and then compare them with what the Gospel teaches us about the Christian virtues. Does such an influence diminish or increase these virtues in us? "A tree is to be judged by its fruits." This is not always easy, because the Devil has it in his interest to hide himself. The saints see the world filled with Devils, and we are continually exposed to their influence.

The *natural spirit (Imit.* III, chap 54) is an enemy of mortification. It seeks its own pleasure even in the supernatural life, and thus falls into spiritual greed (St. John of the Cross). It stops before the first difficulties it meets on the road of virtue, complains of the cross, and becomes irritated. It is indifferent toward the glory of God, toward his Kingdom, and toward the salvation of souls. The *spirit of the Devil* moves us first to exalt ourselves in pride in order that it may then throw us into uneasiness and discouragement. To recognize its influence it is enough to observe it in relation to mortification, humility and the three theological virtues.

It does not necessarily separate us from exterior mortifications. Instead, it sometimes even moves us to an exterior mortification that is exaggerated and obviously visible, thus sustaining our spiritual pride and destroying our health. But it does not move us at all toward the interior mortification of our own will and judgment. On the contrary, it makes us have a great esteem for ourselves, makes us prefer ourselves to others and makes us boast of receiving divine favors. (Arintero adds that it makes us prefer our own Order to other Orders because we are playing a part in it).

This spiritual pride is accompanied by a false humility that makes us speak ill of ourselves to hinder others from doing so and to make them believe in our humility. Instead of nourishing our faith by making us meditate on what is simple in the Gospel, it draws our attention to what is the most extraordinary and often completely extraneous to our vocation. Its scheme for rousing our hope is that of raising within us the presumption of wishing to be perfect saints immediately, without passing through the indispensable stages of detachment. Instead of stirring up our charity, it cultivates self-love in us; instead of bringing us to love our neighbor, it brings us to judge him severely, to be scandalized by his faults and to condemn him. It imitates the zeal of charity by inspiring us with a discontented zeal that always wishes to reprove others and to correct them, instead of correcting ourselves.

All this, instead of generating peace, gives birth to division and hatred. We dare no longer to talk together because we could not stand being contradicted; we no longer see anything but ourselves and we adore ourselves on the pedestal on which we have placed ourselves.

If we commit an offense that is too obvious to hide, we fall into anxiety, discouragement and blindness, and the Devil, who prior to the sin hindered us from seeing the danger, now exaggerates the difficulties in returning to God. After having lifted us up to a proud height, Satan throws us down into spiritual desolation, modeling us to his image just as Our Lord wishes to model us to His.

Therefore, let us be alert! If we feel a great devotion, and yet come from our prayers with a greater amount of self-love, if we have something contrary to our superiors and are not simple in dealing with our spiritual director, then the spirit of evil is in us.

The signs of the *Spirit of God,* however, are absolutely the opposite. This spirit, also, leads us to exterior mortification, yet, in this sense differs from the natural spirit: it promotes an exterior mortification regulated by discretion and obedience which does not tend to make us attract notice or ruin our health. This Spirit of God makes us realize that exterior mortification amounts to very little without a corresponding mortification of the heart, the will, and the judgment—and in this it differs from the spirit of the Devil. It inspires in us a true humility which prohibits us from preferring ourselves to others, does not fear contempt, and keeps silent about its divine favors (which, however, it does not negate or deny, but for which it gives all glory to God).

It nurtures our faith with what is simple and sublime in the Gospel, in conformity with our vocation; it induces us to meditate on the Gospel, aiding us with the traditional interpretation of the

Fathers, without having recourse to hazardous and superficial novelties destined to be soon forgotten. It makes us readily submit to the Supreme Pontiff, to the bishops, our superiors, and our spiritual director. It increases in us the spirit of faith, which makes us see Our Lord in all our legitimate superiors.

It revives our hope without leading us into presumption. It awakens in us a desire for the living waters of mental prayer while keeping us conscious of the fact that this is to be had by passing through successive stages, and that the way along which we must travel is that of humility and the cross.

It increases the fervor of our charity; it infuses zeal for the glory of God and a complete forgetfulness of ourselves. It makes us desire that the name of God be hallowed, that His Kingdom come, that His will be done; and it helps us forget ourselves, leaving the care of ourselves to God, while we think of Him before all else. It gives us love of neighbor, hinders us from making rash judgments about him and of being scandalized by his mistakes. It rouses in us a zeal for the salvation of souls; a zeal, however, that has no bitterness but instead is mild, full of meekness, profoundly humble, discrete, patient, submissive in obedience; a zeal that edifies, above all, by example and prayer and not with inopportune warnings. And this Spirit strengthens our patience in time of trials.

Finally, through all these means the Spirit of God gives us joy and interior peace, peace with ourselves and with others. While the spirit of the Devil builds us up to an immense pride so that we may then be thrown down into despair, the Spirit of God, if we fall, speaks to us of the mercy of our Father instead of exaggerating the difficulties of repentance.

All these signs are described by the Apostle St. Paul (Gal. 5:22–23). In general, they can be reduced to two: simple humility and docility to one's superior and spiritual director. "But we are children of God, and those who know God listen to us; those who are not of God refuse to listen to us. This is how we can tell the spirit of truth from the spirit of falsehood" (1 Jn. 4:6).

If it is no longer a question of the general inspiration of our life, but of a particular act, we must take into account what St. Ignatius and St. John of the Cross say: "It is a sign that it is God who visits the soul when no natural cause has brought us to the profound consolation by which the soul feels itself unexpectedly pervaded." (The Devil can give only superficial joy since he cannot act directly on the intelligence and the will, but only on the imagination and sensibility). We must distinguish with much care, however, the first moment from those which follow, even though the soul may still feel the ardor and the Heavenly favors it has received. In the period of time that follows it often happens that—whether by habit or by our personal way of judging and seeing, or by the inspiration of good or bad inclination—we conceive certain thoughts and form some projects that do not come directly from God. They ought to be first examined with care before they obtain our assent and are put into execution. Hence the necessity again of having recourse to our spiritual director. This made St. Teresa say that the more a soul progresses the more need it has for an enlightened director to distinguish the inspirations of the Holy Spirit that lead it.

To Follow the Voice of the Spirit

When we have recognized the voice of the Holy Spirit, and our superiors and directors have said that we must go forward, we ought no longer to have any hesitation. "The Lord Yahweh has opened my ear. For my part, I made no resistance" (Isa. 50:5). In this way the saints went ahead, despite their trials and the judgments of the world. They knew that God was with them.

Thus Abraham, the father of believers, left his country on the order of God, to go to an unknown country in which, humanly speaking, he could not hope for any hospitality.

Thus St. Paul, on taking leave of the faithful at Miletus said to them: "And now you see me a prisoner already in spirit; I am on my way to Jerusalem, but have no idea what will happen to me there, except that the Holy Spirit, in town after town, has made it clear enough that imprisonment and persecution await me. But life to me is not a thing to waste words on, provided that when I finish my race I have carried out the mission the Lord Jesus gave me—and that was to bear witness to the Good News of God's grace" (Acts 20:22–24).

Thus when Father Michaelis undertook reform in our Order, he proceeded very slowly at the beginning and took all precautions to be certain of what God willed. When he knew God's will, no obstacle placed in his way by a human will could stop him. This man was not guided by his own spirit, but by the Spirit of God. Consequently, we should also conduct ourselves in the same way to reform our personal lives. We should follow the voice of the Holy Spirit as soon as we recognize it. Indeed, every day we say in the Invitatory of Matins: "Today, if you hear His voice, do not harden your hearts."

We ought to walk in the way of humility, faith, hope, and charity in which the Holy Spirit would like to see us run and fly. We should invoke Him with an ardent prayer: "Send forth your Spirit and they will be created, and you will renew the face of the earth" (Ps. 104:30). Then, under the impulse of the Holy Spirit, we will walk like the artist, who, following his own genius, does not think of the rules of art, but observes them only because he possesses their spirit. We will practice all the virtues, even those that are seemingly most opposed: humility and the burning desire of perfection, firmness and meekness, wisdom that sees all in God and prudence that is preoccupied with details. In this way we will have the Spirit of Life.

We should often repeat this sublime prayer of the Church: "Come, Holy Spirit, and from on high send forth the ray of Your light."

CHAPTER XVI

Zeal for the Glory of God and the Salvation of Souls

> *I have come to bring fire on the earth, and how I wish it were blazing already!—Luke 12:49*

WE have seen that love of neighbor is none other than the extension of love of God. Hence, it is a question of one and the same love that is supernatural, theological and essentially divine. In the soul of a religious this love is to become so intense and so ardent as to merit the name of zeal. For a soul consecrated to God it is a duty, an indispensable obligation, to nourish in itself zeal for the glory of God and the salvation of souls. Always it is a question, fundamentally, of the same zeal, of the flame of the one and same love.

The Motive

We ought to make this zeal increase in us because religious profession imposes the obligation of imitating Our Lord, and because we belong to an Order founded essentially for the salvation of souls.

We ought to nourish this zeal if we wish to imitate Our Lord. The dominant virtue of the Sacred Heart is evidently charity, but it is an intense and ardent charity that is likewise a zeal for the glory of God and the salvation of souls. "I have come to bring fire on the earth, and how I wish it were blazing already!"

Our Lord was able to call His zeal for God His food. "My food is to do the will of the One who sent Me" (Jn. 4:34), to glorify the Father, to bring it about that His Name be sanctified, that His Kingdom come, that His will be done. And this will of the Father is precisely the sanctification of souls that are called to know Him, to love Him above everything and to glorify Him in receiving from Him eternal beatitude.

Our Lord was, as it were, devoured by this twofold zeal for God and for souls during His entire life—particularly on the Cross—and He still is in the Eucharist. During His life He manifested the Name of God to men, revealed God as a Father of all peoples without distinction of class or nation; He revealed God to us as a light which, coming into this world, illumines every man and takes pleasure especially in illuminating the small and the humble; He revealed God to us as love and mercy, ever looking over us to heal us. He proclaimed the rights of God as the foundation of all justice, and in the first place God's right of being known, loved and glorified.

He declared that the gravest of all evils was the insult made to His Father who is infinitely good. This insult, whose infinite gravity in its total extension into the past and future He penetrated and felt, was the great suffering of His life. If sons instinctively suffer because of an offense made to their father, how much did Our Lord have to suffer—especially when He saw that this offense came from us whom He wished to save!

He willed to offer Himself as a victim in our place to make reparation and obtain for us pardon. On the Cross He took upon Himself the iniquities of all enemies, His Own and His Father's; He suffered for all our sins as if He had been guilty —He who was devoured by a burning thirst for the glory of God. And this indescribable suffering He offered to His Father for us, making to God a reparation as great as God Himself. This insult could not cease to exist until men separated from God had been led back to Him for their salvation and His glory; for this reason, on the Cross He had a thirst for our souls, even to the point of dying for them.

When St. Catherine of Siena asked Him, "My Lord, what was your greatest pain, that of the body or that of desire?" Jesus replied to her with infinite tenderness: "My child, there can be no comparison between something finite and something infinite. Consider that the pain of My body was limited, while My desire for the salvation of souls was infinite. This burning thirst, this cross of desire, I felt all My life. It was more painful for Me than all the pains that I bore in My body. Nevertheless, My soul was moved with joy seeing the final moment approach, especially at the supper of Holy Thursday when I said, 'I have desired ardently to eat this Pasch with you,' that is, sacrifice My body to My Father. I had a great joy, a great consolation, because I saw the time arrive when this cross of desire would cease for Me; and the closer I felt Myself to the flagellation and the other torments of My body, the more I felt the pain in Me diminish. The pain of the body made that of desire disappear, because I saw completed what I had desired. With death on the Cross the pain of the holy desire ended, but not the desire and the hunger I have for your salvation. If this love that I have for you were extinguished, you would no longer exist, since it is only this love that maintains you in life."

In the Eucharist there is the same zeal for God and for mankind. On the altar and in the tabernacle, Jesus is the most excellent Adorer of the Majesty of His Father. Thus, even in the smallest village God is adored without an instant of interruption. Night and day, when the faithful are working or resting, there is One who does not cease in rendering to God worship and adoration worthy of Him, because Our Lord, always living, does not cease to intercede for us and to offer Himself as victim to make reparation for our offenses. In this same Sacrament of love, the Sacred Heart expresses to us its thirst for our souls. Every day He offers Himself to us as food, to sanctify us more and more and to assimilate us to Himself.

"My delights are among the sons of men" (Prov. 8:31). He asks us for our love as if He had need of us, whereas it is we who can do nothing without Him. He becomes the support and consolation of thousands of fervent souls, from the missionary who exposes himself to death that he might spread the Gospel, to the humble Christian woman who, obliged to live in the world and sometimes in very perverse surroundings, comes to seek every morning in Holy Communion the strength to defend herself from the temptations that surround her.

Our religious profession enjoins us to imitate this ardent zeal of Our Lord. St. Catherine of Siena said: "I should like to see you suffer so much from hunger for the salvation of souls that you would be able to die for them as Christ Jesus or, at least, that you might die perfectly to the world and to yourselves."

We ought to nourish this zeal also because we belong to an Order founded essentially for the salvation of men. We should recall the example of our father, St. Dominic: his incessant prayer, his nocturnal flagellations and his continual preaching in the midst of the greatest difficulties provoked by the heretics.

This ardent zeal made him say to his enemies, from whom he had unwittingly escaped: "If you had captured me, I would have begged you not to kill me with one blow, but to cut off my members one by one, and after putting the mutilated pieces before me, to finish by snatching out my eyes and leaving me immersed in my blood." The whole heart of St. Dominic is in this heroic cry, which reminds us of the ardor of the great martyr, St. Ignatius of Antioch, who desired to be chewed and devoured by the wild beasts for the glory of Jesus Christ. We should recall the zeal of St. Catherine of Siena for some persons who generally did not thank her except with insult and slander.

The Extension

We must direct this zeal in a particular way to the salvation of those in our homeland. In increasing numbers these people are separated from God and Christ. Without faith, hope and charity they have no other concern than pleasures of the world and their fortunes. They drink iniquity like water with almost no awareness, and they run with indifference toward damnation. An immense multitude of poor, misled people amuse themselves on the brink of an abyss that at any moment can swallow them up for eternity. Meanwhile, some extremely perverse individuals, with a perversity worse than merely human, furiously persist with all means to deprive the little ones of the light of life and the bread of life.

We should often think about this militant Church that is our mother. The war that is waged against her is hateful, terrible in its consequences, entirely different from every other war, without anything human about it. A war of the spirit, loaded with heavy responsibilities, profound, terrible and hateful like the sins of the spirit, a war that is waged in the inner recesses of the heart between Our Lord and the Devil. And therein is found the whole history of the world.

The Church sees the eternal consequences for those who wage this war against her, yet she continues to love them as sons and to pray that God will cure them of their blindness and stop them on the road to eternal damnation where their fury drives them. Upon us, fellow religious, devolves the task of making reparation by loving our Mother, the Church, with all our spirit, with the most complete submission, with all our heart, with all our soul, and with all our strength.

Our zeal must extend likewise to the Church in purgatory. This Church is for us truly our neighbor. We ought to assist the suffering members of Christ and give them relief because we all belong to the same body. These souls, who are our brothers and sisters, find themselves in indescribable torments, suffering both the pain of loss and of the senses.

St. Catherine de Ricci suffered this pain of the senses for a soul for whom she offered herself. A mysterious flame was lighted in her body. From her head to her feet were formed blisters filled with boiling water and when these were absorbed the body of the saint seemed parched with fire. She remained in her cell which became like an oven, painfully enduring the heat. This torment lasted forty days when it suddenly ended.

But the souls of purgatory suffer above all else the pain of the loss of, or rather the privation of, God. Here below this privation does not make us suffer because this is our condition. For the souls in purgatory it is different because they should already be seeing God. They have arrived at the end of their voyage, are separated from the world, are deprived of their consolations, diversions and every means of being able to merit. All that is in them urges them toward a God whom they should, but do not, possess. They find themselves, as it were, suspended between two worlds. Their life goes on, no longer to merit, but to suffer. They are completely immersed in suffering, and they think of nothing else. St Augustine and St. Thomas both affirm that the smallest of their pains is greater than all those that can be experienced in this world. Yet, all these souls are holy, temples of the Holy Spirit, members of Christ, incapable of sin in the sufferings they bear for love of divine justice.

These souls wait for our help, our alms. They no longer can merit, but we can merit for them. They no longer can gain indulgences, while we, with a bit of good will and the spirit of faith, can gain indulgences for them by drawing from the infinite treasury of the Church, thus hastening their liberation. These are the motives of our zeal, which should be extended to all souls.

How Is This Zeal to Be Exercised?

This zeal is to be exercised according to the example of Our Lord, of St. Dominic, and of St. Catherine of Siena. This means, by prayer, by penance, and by the spiritual and corporal works of mercy which our rule imposes on us. Today many works of all types are undertaken, but often the very soul of these works is forgotten: prayer and penance. Our Lady of Lourdes, in the nineteenth century, a century so proud of its attainments, found nothing more necessary to say than: "Pray and do penance."

Prayer is the true and most powerful instrument of action being the first condition and the soul of the apostolic life. Works without prayer are sterile, because it is grace that acts on souls and grace is attained by prayer: "Ask and you will receive." The apostolate of prayer must constantly support that of word and of action. The humble lay sister kneeling at the foot of the Crucifix can obtain much more by her prayer than a preacher of great talent who does not pray. Talent by itself does nothing but make a bit of noise. "It is only a tinkling cymbal," as St. Paul says (1 Cor. 13:1), while prayer, even alone, without skill and talent, accomplishes wonders and is capable of moving mountains.

It was revealed to St. Teresa that, by her prayer at the foot of the Crucifix, she had converted as many souls as St. Francis Xavier, the Apostle of India, who traveled through the whole world carrying the word of God. We should remember that the prayer which St. Stephen, the first martyr, spoke as he ascended into Heaven, offered on behalf of those stoning him, drew down grace on the soul of St. Paul who was guarding the cloaks of those fanatics.

We ought to recall the force of the prayer of St. Peter Martyr when, no longer able to preach, breathing his last and bathed in his own blood, he ardently prayed for his executioner. The prayer of St. Peter Martyr converted that brutal soul, which up to that time had known only the vilest and most violent passions, into the soul of a saint. So intense was the light that illuminated the spirit of that wretched man, so penetrating was the contrition that overturned his heart, that he bitterly wept over his crime, asked for the Dominican habit and spent forty years in the practice of the most heroic virtues and most rigorous penance. He edified his confreres and the entire city to such a point that they all called him "the blessed one." He died a saint and his remains were venerated. This is the force of prayer for the salvation of souls! Let us pray, then, that the preaching of our confreres bears good fruit.

That charming, gracious Carmelite, St. Therese of the Child Jesus, hidden in her monastery, by her prayers made the apostolate of two missionaries of India fruitful by preparing souls to receive their word and keep it.

We should also pray for the souls in purgatory, of whom we spoke earlier. It would be so easy to seek to gain for them the plenary indulgences on the feast days of our saints and all the other indulgences that the Church in her solicitude deigns to concede for the benefit of these poor souls. The question here is not of accomplishing "the heroic act" of applying all our meritorious acts to the total benefit of these souls. If we wish to despoil ourselves in this way, we should think it over thoroughly and seek counsel, and take into account what we are giving and what we are renouncing, and what a terrible increase of pain may be its inevitable consequence. We must be assured that this act of generosity does not have its origin in an enthusiastic imagination, but rather in charity and the inspiration of God.

Hence, it is not fitting to make such a renunciation without the consent of our spiritual director.

Some prefer to let Our Lord dispose of their acts of satisfaction and their merits without first determining how He should dispose of them. Without coming to this point, there are so many merits and sacrifices we can offer every day to hasten the liberation of these souls! In any case, prayer is always fruitful. Holy persons cannot render it sterile, as can sinners, who can always refuse to be converted.

In addition to prayer, the zeal of St. Dominic added penance for those who do no penance and mortification for those who do not mortify themselves. The perfect, in imitation of Christ, are to redeem souls with their blood. As St. Theresa writes: "The religious who comes into the convent solely to expiate her sins—I don't understand what on earth she is doing!"

In sanctifying ourselves we are to sanctify our brethren too. A great means of sanctification, together with prayer, is the cross. When we crucify our body, Our Lord can spare some poor sick body—sick, perhaps through its own fault and with little strength left—or the body of a poor man who needs his health to earn bread for his children. When we immolate our heart to God, Our Lord can cure a sick heart that lacks strength to break its chains. When we immolate our will to God, Our Lord raises up a dead will. These are the two great means of exercising our zeal for the salvation of others: prayer and penance.

To these, however, we must add the spiritual and corporal works of mercy as well as those imposed by our rule: Christian instruction and education, education given by example and word. We have the splendid mission of forming the Christian spirit, of forming hearts and wills to the love of God and neighbor and—why not say it?—of forming and generating Jesus Christ in the souls of children, who were loved so much by Our Lord.

Thus, later, they may shine in the world like the small "city built on the mountain" of which Our Lord speaks (Mt. 5:14).

The importance of this mission becomes greater in the age we are going through today, when almost "all truth has vanished from among the sons of man" (Ps. 12:2)—the truths of God, the excess of His love, His indefeasible rights and the rigor of His justice, the truths regarding the great duties toward father and mother, toward country, toward the poor of Christ.

We have the mission of molding these children to self-denial, to humility, to the spirit of faith and charity. We have the mission of revealing to them the worship and adoration of the Sacred Heart and of the Blessed Virgin, the mission of teaching them that the rich man must consider himself solely an administrator of the goods of God and must help those who are dying of hunger, instead of aggravating them with his egoism, his luxury and his insatiable need of enjoyment. This is the sublime mission, blessed by God, if we consider that the child is like a spring and as we make the spring, so will be the stream, that is, the family. Where will this which we begin reach? Only God knows. This zeal must always be accompanied by prudence and tempered by humility and meekness, but without ceasing to be ardent.

Lord, give us this zeal, the dominant virtue of your Sacred Heart, the virtue of our blessed father St. Dominic. Teach us to pray ardently for souls that are lost, teach us to carry the cross for them because You have conceded us immense graces they have not received. Make our sufferings, supported in union with You, diminish the blindness of sinners and move their heart. Lord, give us this thirst for souls even to the point of dying for them, as you died for them; or, certainly, to the point of truly dying to ourselves to live eternally in You with these souls!

CHAPTER XVII

Devotion to the Blessed Virgin

Son, behold thy Mother—John 19:27

WE cannot preach a retreat to religious, and above all to contemplative religious, without dedicating a discourse to the great devotion we ought to have toward the Mother of God. Therefore, I should like to speak of the Virgin Mary, our Mother and our Mediatrix, being inspired above all by the doctrine of a saint whom we know very well, St. Louis Grignon de Montfort, author of the book *True Devotion to Mary.*[1]

This profitable work was found under a layer of dust only after the French Revolution. Since then, the book has been translated into all the major languages. I believe that this is the book that has contributed most in spreading the doctrine of the universal mediation of the Blessed Virgin. This doctrine had existed previously. Father Olier recalled it and taught it to his first sons, and they in turn, trained St. Louis Grignon. It was the latter who received infused contemplation of the mystery of the Blessed Virgin, and when he wrote on this subject he could continue at great length because he spoke from the abundance of his heart. This small tract is a treasure for the Church, as is indeed its summary, entitled *The Secret of Mary*, which the Saint made for a sister religious.

---

1 Publisher's note: For additional information on Marian Consecration and the four Marian dogmas, see *33 Days to Morning Glory* by Fr. Michael Gaitley, MIC and *Meet Your Mother* by Dr. Mark Miravalle, both available from Lighthouse Catholic Media.

He says first of all that he is concerned with devotion to Mary and seeks to demonstrate its principal levels and the heights to which it should reach. He begins with the observation that the Protestants wished to deny the mediation of Mary, while the Jansenists wanted to diminish it. He comments on some Catholics who had allowed themselves to be influenced: "Also among the Catholics there are some who know the Virgin Mary only in a speculative way. They fear that in their devotion to the Holy Virgin they may be trespassing, that they may be injuring their devotion to Our Lord." They seem to believe that Mary is an obstacle to attaining divine union, whereas in reality she exercises all her influence to lead us to the most intimate union with her Son.

When we approach the Virgin, we are indeed approaching a person in whom Our Lord was pleased and in whom the Holy Trinity dwells and reigns most profoundly. To approach her, means to approach her Son and her Heavenly Father. We will analyze the question, then, by dividing the subject into the following three points: why we should have great devotion to Mary; how we should practice it; and what are its fruits.

Why We Should Have a Great Devotion to the Holy Virgin

Theology tells us that for Mary we ought to have not only a veneration of *dulia* such as is owed to the saints, but a veneration of *hyperdulia*. *Hyperdulia*, in fact, comes immediately after the worship and adoration of *latria* which is reserved for God, and for the divine humanity of Our Savior inasmuch as it is united to the Person of the Word and is the sensible instrument of His immense love.

But why should we render a veneration of *hyperdulia* to Mary? If she were only "full of grace" and not also the Mother of God, would there have to be a veneration of *hyperdulia* for her? The greater part of the theologians respond negatively and the

Congregation of Rites is fully in agreement with them on this point. Therefore, it is only because she is the Mother of God that she is owed this veneration, and not because she is full of grace. If she were full of grace without being the Mother of God we would not render her a special veneration. Such worship is owed her by reason of her divine maternity. This latter is of an order that not only surpasses the natural order, but even the order of grace and glory because it has recourse to the hypostatic order constituted by the very mystery of the Incarnation.

Mary is the Mother of Jesus who is God, and for this reason her motherhood terminates in the very Person of the Incarnate Word and reaches to the very boundaries of Divinity. Mary is the Mother of Jesus who is God. Certainly, she did not give Him His divine nature, but only His human nature. She is Mother, however, not precisely by reason of the humanity of Jesus, but by reason of the Incarnate Word because motherhood terminates not in a nature, but in the person possessing this nature: in this case in the very Person of the Word.

The Most Holy Virgin, since she conceived Him corporeally and spiritually, is His Mother in two ways: (1) corporeally, since He is flesh of her flesh, and the torch of His human life was kindled in the womb of the Virgin by the work of the Holy Spirit; and (2) spiritually, inasmuch as the formal consent of the Virgin was necessary so that the Word might be united in her to our nature and the mystery of the Incarnation be fulfilled in this way. From all eternity God had decreed to concede to Mary a grace that would let her say her *fiat*[2] to the Incarnation. And she said it with greatest humility, with faith and courage because from the book of Isaiah she had learned what the sufferings of Our Lord would be.

---

2 Editor's note: In Luke 1:26–38 the angel Gabriel appears to Mary and shares God's desire for her to virginally conceive the long awaited Savior. Mary gives her "yes" or *fiat* (Latin for "let it be done") and the Son of God becomes incarnate in her womb.

This dignity of the Mother of God, being of the hypostatic order, surpasses that of all the saints together. Now it is precisely in view of this motherhood that Mary has received all the privileges that were conceded to her. God has bestowed all these privileges on her that she might be the worthy Mother of Our Lord. She had been predestined, in the first place, to the divine Motherhood and in view of this Motherhood, to a very high degree of grace and glory—so much so that the initial grace she received at the instant of her Immaculate Conception already surpassed the final grace of all the saints together. This follows since, as the Fathers say, God loved the Holy Virgin as His future Mother already at the instant of her conception. This love for her, greater than that which He had for all creatures and for all the angels together, produced in her a proportionate grace. If, therefore, the Virgin alone was loved more than all the hierarchies of the angels, then she had received from the first instant an initial fullness of grace and charity that surpasses the final grace of all the saints.

To understand this better, we can make use of some analogies. A most beautiful diamond is worth much more than many ordinary gems. It is said that the founder of an Order, in view of the Order he is to found and for which he has received a special inspiration, is worth more than all his companions combined. It is said also that St. Thomas by himself is worth more than all his commentators together, because he received a grace of illumination that permitted him to see better than others the questions he solved. He saw them from a point of view that was higher and in a way more universal; so his authority prevails. Consequently, we need not be surprised if Pius XI said that "the initial fullness of grace in Mary already surpasses the sum total of grace of all the saints together before their entrance into glory."

In the moment in which she received this fullness, Mary was preserved from original sin because it was necessary that the perfect Redeemer Jesus Christ exercise a sovereign redemption, at least with regard to the one soul that would be most intimately associated with Him in the work of redemption. If a doctor were to succeed not only in helping someone recover from a mortal wound, but in preventing its occurrence, it could be said that he is a savior in the natural order. In this sense is Our Lord the Savior of His Mother. The Holy Virgin was preserved from original sin because of the merits of her Son, and for the purpose of becoming His worthy Mother. From that instant, grace, with charity and the virtues, increased in her soul in magnificent crescendo until her death.

Just as bodies fall faster the closer they come to earth, so souls in the state of grace ought to advance faster toward God the closer they come to Him and are drawn by Him. This is realized in the saints toward the end of their lives. But this marvelous law of acceleration is realized above all in the Holy Virgin because in her there was no longer anything that could slow down the movement of her ascent toward God: neither original sin, nor any personal sin, nor any imperfection of the will. Consequently, in her there was a marvelous progress, an acceleration more and more pronounced. Here below, the Virgin by herself had greater power than all the saints together, so much more that the saints can do nothing without her help; she is truly the universal Mediatrix.

The reason why we owe this veneration to Mary derives, therefore, from the fact that she is the Mother of God, and to be such she received the fullness of grace and all privileges. She will always remain, in Heaven just as on earth, the worthy Mother of Our Lord, and Our Lord in Heaven will honor her as His Mother.

Mary is our Mother and universal Mediatrix. She is our Mother above all because she gives us the Author of Grace. She is *Mater Salvatoris*. By that very fact she is already our Mediatrix since it is through her and her *fiat* that Jesus was given to the world as Our Savior, brother and victim.

She became still more our Mother (and she was proclaimed such) when she became more perfectly our Co-redemptrix, uniting herself more intimately than anyone else to the sacrifice of Jesus. It is taught in the Church today that all that Jesus merited for us in justice, the Holy Virgin merited for us by a merit of fittingness *(de congruo)*. While Jesus satisfied for us in justice, she satisfied in fittingness, and by this she became our Mother. She became our Mother through an act of faith superior to that which the saints made when they were wayfarers on this earth.

The greatest faith that has ever existed is that of Mary. Our Lord, in fact, did not have faith but the Beatific Vision. The greatest act of faith of which Mary was capable took place on Calvary: she did not cease believing that Jesus was the Incarnate Word of God, was victorious over the Devil and sin, and that He would conquer death.

She became our Mother, however, not only by this act of faith, but also by the greatest act of hope performed on earth. Jesus, of course, did not have to hope, since He was God Himself.

Finally, she became our Mother through the greatest act of love that she could make at that moment: she loved God to the point of offering Him her Son in the midst of the greatest torments. She felt in her own heart all the physical and moral sufferings of Our Lord in a measure corresponding to her love for God whom sinners offend, for her Son whom sin will crucify and for our souls which sin ruins and kills. Just as we cannot fathom the fullness of the Holy Virgin's charity, so we cannot appreciate the fullness of her suffering. As Bossuet says, "one and the same Cross was sufficient for her and Him since she also was, we could say, nailed on the Cross of her Son. Here is the strength of her love: for Him she suffered the same sufferings."

In her suffering, she brought us forth to the life of grace. It was accomplished in that painful moment when Our Lord said to the Holy Virgin: "Woman, behold your son," committing her to St. John. Since the eighth century the Church has taught that St. John personified all the souls that were to be redeemed by the sacrifice of the Cross. Those words of Christ were certainly not directed to St. John alone. They denote in St. John all the souls that would be redeemed by the Cross. This is their spiritual sense. These words, as a sacramental word, produce what they signify: they produce in the soul of the Virgin a considerable increase of charity and of maternal charity toward us, while they produced in St. John's soul a wholly filial affection, full of respect toward the Mother of God.

From that moment the irradiation of the spiritual maternity of the Holy Virgin begins. This irradiation will not cease until the end of the world, because even after she ascended into Heaven she continues to be our Mediatrix, to intercede for us and concede us all our graces. She does not cease to pray for us. We have a proof of this in tradition, as in the Litany of Loreto: "Health of the Sick" and "Comforter of the Afflicted." All graces are therefore transmitted to us through her who obtains them for us.

By the word "now" of the Hail Mary, we are seeking the grace of the present moment, the most necessary of all graces since the grace of the present moment is the most useful of all. When we asked for it, we may have been very distracted, but the Holy Virgin is not. Thus, when we have received it, we can be certain that it was through the intercession of Mary. She is the distributor of all graces including sacramental grace, since she often sends the confessor to the dying sinner so that attrition may be transformed into contrition. We should also ask her to dispose our soul for a worthy Holy Communion.

We thus see that the influence of the Holy Virgin, far from impeding union with Our Lord, leads us instead to a more and more profound union with her Son. Consequently, without a very great union with the Holy Virgin, we cannot attain an intimate union with Our Lord. Among other things, it would be a lack of humility to slight the mediators that the good Lord has given us because of our weakness. Intimacy with the Lord in prayer will be greatly facilitated by a frequent recourse to the Holy Virgin.

How to Practice This Devotion

St. Louis Grignon speaks of three levels of this devotion. It is not strange that he makes such distinctions for all the infused virtues really increase with the increase of charity. The first level is that of beginners; the second, that of those who have made some progress; and the third, that of the perfect. An increase arises in proportion to the virtue of religion and the gift of piety.

We will speak, then, of these three levels of this devotion which ought to exist in all Christians and should increase with charity. The first level, that of beginners, consists in praying now and again to the Virgin, honoring her as the Mother of God, reciting, for example, with great recollection the *Angelus* whenever we hear it sounded. The second level, that of those who have made some progress, consists of having more perfect sentiments of veneration, of confidence and of love toward Mary. This brings one to say the Rosary every day, or at least one of the three parts of the Rosary, meditating on the joyful, sorrowful, or glorious mysteries which are for us the way to eternal life. He who recites the holy Rosary well belongs to a school of contemplation. (Our Lord manifested Himself to St. Teresa in the mysteries of His infancy.) If we say the Rosary well, Our Lord comes to us. Therefore, it is sufficient to fix our gaze upon Him while our lips repeat the song of the Hail Marys and our fingers tell the beads. This produces in our soul an increase of grace in proportion to our devotion.

The third level of devotion to Mary, that which belongs to the perfect, consists in being wholly consecrated to Our Lord through her hands. St. Louis Grignon de Montfort explains very well what this means: "This devotion consists in giving oneself fully to Our Lord through Mary. We must give her (1) our body with all its senses and members, that she preserve it in a perfect purity; (2) our soul with all its potencies; (3) our present and future eternal goods; (4) our interior and spiritual goods which are our merits, our virtues, and our good works of the past, present and future." To understand this offering well, we must clearly distinguish in our good works what is incommunicable and what is communicable to other souls.

What is incommunicable in our good works is merit properly termed *de condigno.* This constitutes a right in justice to an increase of charity and to eternal life. These personal merits are incommunicable. They differ from the merits of Our Lord in that He, being the constituted head of humanity, was able to merit for us in strict, rigorous justice. Consequently, if we offer these merits to the Holy Virgin, it is not for her to give them to other souls, but for her to preserve them and make them fruitful. Thus, if we should have the disgrace of losing them by mortal sin, she may obtain for us the grace of a fervent contrition which enables us to regain not only the state of grace but also the level of grace lost. In that way, if we have lost five talents, we are able to find five, and not just two or three.

What is communicable in our good works is the merit of fittingness *(de congruo),* and in addition their value of satisfaction or reparation and their value of petition or prayer.

With a merit of fittingness, founded not on justice but on the charity or friendship which unites us to God *in jure amicabili,* we are able to obtain graces for our neighbor. Thus a good Christian mother draws graces on her children by her virtuous life because God considers the intentions and good works of this generous mother. In the same way, we can pray for the conversion and spiritual progress of our neighbor, for hardened sinners, for those in agony, and for the souls in purgatory. Finally, we can satisfy for others and expiate for them as Mary did for us at the foot of the Cross, thus drawing upon them the divine mercy. In the same way, we are able to earn indulgences for the souls in purgatory, to open to them the treasure of merits of Our Lord Jesus Christ and the saints, and thereby hasten their liberation.

If we offer to Mary all our pains and tribulations, she will send us crosses proportionate to our strength, sustained by grace, to make us collaborators in the salvation of souls.

To whom is it fitting to counsel such a consecration? There is no point of counseling this to those who would be doing it out of sentimentality or spiritual pride without understanding its fuller meaning. On the other hand, it is fitting to counsel it to persons truly pious and fervent; it can be counseled at the beginning for brief periods, perhaps in relation to the feasts of the Virgin, and then for a year. In this way they will be gradually pervaded by this spirit of abandonment, and eventually they will be able to make this act fruitful for their entire lives.

Sometimes an objection is advanced. "But this means despoiling ourselves of what is our own and not paying our debts, a thing that will increase our purgatory." The Devil made this objection to St. Bridget when she was disposed to making such an act. Our Lord let her understand that this objection derives from self-love which forgets the goodness of Mary: our celestial Mother does not allow herself to be outdone in generosity. By emptying ourselves in this way we receive the hundredfold. This generous act attests to love itself, which already obtains for us the remission of a part of our purgatory.

Other persons object. "But as a result, how can we pray specifically for our relatives and friends if we have once committed for all time all our merits and prayers to Mary?" To this objection we must reply that the Holy Virgin knows our obligations in charity toward our relatives and friends, and when we forget to pray for them according to our duty, it will be precisely she who remembers them. Moreover, among our relatives and friends there are some who have a particular need of prayer. We are often ignorant of this, yet the Holy Virgin knows it well. Thus she is able, even without our awareness, to allow these souls to benefit from our prayer. For the other persons, meanwhile, we can always ask her to favor them.

The Fruits of This Devotion

St. Louis Grignon de Montfort affirms that this way of going to God is *easier,* and also *more meritorious*—and consequently it is a more perfect way, shorter and more secure. Above all it is, as he says, an easier way: "One can in truth attain divine union through other ways; but it will be with many crosses, with more profound annihilation of self, and with difficulties that we shall overcome with greater effort. It will be necessary to pass through dark nights, through pricking thorns and horrible deserts. On the other hand, through the way of Mary we advance more gently and calmly. There are found, it is true, great battles to engage in and great difficulties to overcome; but this good Mother comes close to her faithful in such a way that she enlightens them in their darkness, illumines them in their doubts, sustains them in their battles and difficulties. Indeed, this purest (virginal) way of finding Jesus Christ is a way of roses and honey in comparison to other ways."

This can be observed in the lives of the saints who have followed this way more specifically, such as St. Ephraim, St. John of Damascus, St. Bernard, St. Bonaventure, St. Bernadine of Siena, St. Francis de Sales, and many others. We know the vision of St. Francis of Assisi. One day he saw his sons trying to climb up toward Our Lord on a red-colored ladder, set at a very steep incline; after having climbed several steps, they fell down. Then Our Lord showed St. Francis another ladder, of white color and with a much slighter incline, at whose top stood the Holy Virgin. Then He said to him: "Recommend to your sons that they go up on My Mother's ladder."

It is a more facile way because the Virgin sustains us with her gentleness; and it is *more meritorious* because Mary obtains for us a greater charity, which is the principle of merit. Indeed the difficulties to overcome are certainly an occasion of merit; but the principle of merit is in charity, in love of God, with which we triumph in these very difficulties. We ought to be convinced that Mary merits more by her more facile acts—as by a simple prayer—than the martyrs with their torments, since she accomplishes these simple acts with a love of God that is greater than that with which the saints accomplish their most heroic acts. Mary's way, being more facile, is also more meritorious, shorter, more perfect, more secure. Walking an easier way, we advance more quickly. We advance more rapidly by submitting ourselves to the Mother of God than by confiding excessively in our personal prudence. Under the direction of her whom the Incarnate Word obeyed, one walks with giant steps.

This way is also *more perfect* because, as through Mary the Word descended perfectly to us without losing anything of His divinity, in the same way, by means of her the smallest persons can ascend perfectly to the Most High without fear. She purifies our good works and increases their value in presenting them to her Son.

Finally, it is a *more secure* way because in it we are preserved to a great degree from the seductions of him who seeks to deceive us and push us imperceptibly into grave sin. Moreover, on this way we are better protected from illusions of foolish fancy and sentimentality. Indeed, in the interplay of causes that permit the transmission of divine grace, Mary exercises a salutary influence over our sensibility, calming and regulating it, in such a manner as to permit the superior part of the soul to receive more fruitfully the influence of Our Lord. Moreover, for our sensibility, Mary is in herself a most pure and most holy object which elevates our soul toward union with God.

She gives us a great interior liberty and sometimes she obtains for us immediately—when we ask her with insistence—a liberation from the deviations of our sensibility which hinder prayer and intimate union with Our Lord.

The whole influence of Mary as a Mediatrix has as its purpose to conduct us to intimacy with Jesus, just as He Himself leads us to His Father. Fittingly we ask this particular assistance of Mary at Holy Communion that she may allow us to participate in her profound devotion and in her love just as if she were giving us her most pure heart with which to receive worthily Our Lord. And it is fitting to make our thanksgiving in the same manner.

To conclude, let us repeat here the essence of our consecration to Jesus through the hand of Mary:

> O eternal and uncreated wisdom, O most lovable and adorable Jesus, true God and true man, I thank you for having emptied Yourself, taking on the form of a slave to liberate me from the slavery of the Devil.
>
> I run to the intercession of Your most holy Mother whom You have given me as a Mediatrix, and through whom I hope to obtain from You contrition and pardon for my sins, to acquire and preserve wisdom.

I salute you Mary Immaculate, Queen of Heaven and earth, to whose command all that is under God is submitted.

I salute you, O secure refuge of sinners, whose mercy fails no one; hear the desire that I have for divine wisdom and receive the vows and the offerings that my littleness presents to you.

I, an unfaithful sinner, renew and ratify today into your hands the promises of my baptism: I renounce forever Satan, his works and his pomps, and I give myself entirely to Jesus Christ, Incarnate Wisdom, to carry behind Him my cross all the days of my life.

And to be more faithful to Him than I have been up till today, I choose you, O Mary, for my Mother. I give and consecrate to you my body and my soul, my interior and exterior goods, and the value of my actions, past, present, and future. Present me to your Son, grant me the grace to obtain the true Wisdom of God and admit me, for this reason, into the number of those whom you love, instruct, lead, nourish, and protect.

O faithful Virgin, make of me a perfect disciple, imitator of Incarnate Wisdom, Jesus Christ, your Son; make me attain, by your intercession and example, the fullness of His age on earth, and the fullness of His glory in Heaven.

CHAPTER XVIII

Union with God

> *Shoulder My yoke and learn from Me,*
> *for I am gentle and humble in heart,*
> *and you will find rest for your souls—*
> *Matthew 11:29*

WE have seen what the experiential knowledge of God in mental prayer is, what love of God and neighbor ought to be as well as what ought to be our zeal for the glory of God and for the salvation of souls. The aim of this experiential knowledge and of this love, the end of the interior life here below, is union with God, a union still imperfect but which is the principle and pledge of perfect union that awaits us in Heaven. This union is the repose of the soul in God, who is found and makes Himself always felt in this union, even in labors and sufferings. We will see what this union with God is and what the means are to attain it.

What Is This Union?

What is this presence of God in us which permits us to repose in Him? First of all, it is certain that God is present in us as in all things which He conserves in existence and to which He gives motion. If the divine action were to cease to sustain things, they would, in fact, return to nothingness in the same way that darkness comes when the sun goes down.

But the Lord speaks of a presence in us wholly special when he says: "If anyone loves Me he will keep My word, and My Father will love him, and we shall come to him and make our home with him" (Jn. 14:23). If someone loves Me with a love that is not only affective but also effective and operative, by keeping My words in his heart and observing My commandments, the Father and I will come to him and make our abode with him, conversing with him as friend to friend. Indeed, it is a property of love that he who loves is united to the object loved by him (S.T. I-II, q. 28, a. 1). Love urges one to seek the presence of the loved one, or at least to converse with him in one's thoughts. According to St. Augustine, love is the good that unites those who love one another. They are present one to another with a presence that is at least affective, and much more intimate than the simple union of bodies. If such is the property of love in general, and even that of an inferior type of love, what will be the property of charity, supernatural love, or above all of charity that attains the summit of perfection?

God, already present in us really and substantially, as He is in all things whose being He conserves, makes Himself present in us in a special way when His Spirit of Love communicates to us divine charity—a participation of the love that unites the divine Persons among themselves. God is present in all the souls in the state of grace, not only as a cause united to its effect, but He abides there as in a spiritual temple in which He is known and loved. God dwells in this spiritual temple even when we sleep; but He is truly known and loved when the soul makes an act of faith and charity and when, with the gift of Wisdom, the Holy Spirit makes Himself felt in the soul as the life of its life. Every time, then, that a believing soul merits an increase of grace and charity by its fervor and generosity, the Holy Spirit becomes still more present in it with this presence of knowledge and love (S.T. I, q. 43, a. 6 ad 2).

Under the influence of a superior light, the soul attains in this way a sentiment of the presence of God so vivid and profound that it cannot doubt this divine presence. Hence it now "feels" God so to speak; and this new experience becomes for it truly that repose of the soul of which Our Lord speaks. Though still remaining in the obscurity of faith, the soul already possesses the beginning of the happiness of Heaven. The soul feels itself penetrated by God as incandescent iron is penetrated by fire, or as the air is penetrated by the rays of the sun.

Although this union is never a transformation that absorbs the soul into God as some false mystics have pretended, it is true, however, that the soul feels God in its most intimate recesses. In a certain sense, God is more intimate to the soul than the soul itself, inasmuch as He is the interior principle of its whole inner life. This union which brings the gifts of the Holy Spirit urges from within the accomplishment of acts that the soul by itself could not accomplish.

Such a constant union is realized in contemplation, and though the false mystics say the contrary, it cannot be permanent: the weakness of our nature often forces us to interrupt it, at least during sleep *(S.T.* I-II, q. 3, a. 2 ad 4). In the more perfect souls, God manifests His presence more continuously: it is a question of a confused feeling of the presence of God and of a state of perfect habitual docility to all His inspirations. Uninterrupted union is not of this world; it is the condition of the saints in Heaven.

This union with God has many degrees, as do charity and the gifts of the Holy Spirit. The most exalted of them is the spiritual marriage of which Sacred Scripture, the Fathers, and the great mystics speak; it is a marriage in comparison to which earthly marriage is only a symbol. Like earthly marriage, it procures three worthy objectives: reciprocal fidelity, indissolubility, and the posterity of good works. The soul that receives such a great favor, however, is not at all certain of its own salvation nor of being preserved from every fall. "It is secure only," says St. Teresa, "when Our Lord leads it by the hand and it does not offend Him." "The bride," says St. Lawrence Justinian, "ought to strive to be faithful and for fear of backsliding it ought never to believe that it has attained the summit of perfection." Spiritual marriage, ratified on earth by good works, will be consummated only in Heaven, where the continuity and indissolubility of union will be perfect.

Though it is less perfect, earthly union with God sometimes surpasses that of some blessed ones in Heaven: the apostle St. John had on earth a degree of charity and union with God which was more exalted than that which a baby, taken by death immediately after baptism, possesses in Heaven. Even without seeing Him, the apostle St. John loved God in an intimate manner, just as we are able to love certain persons living far from us more than those we see every day.

Concerning this union with God here below, one can have only moral certitude. As long as he lives on earth, unless one has a special revelation, he cannot know with certainty whether he is worthy of love or hate (cf. Eccles. 9:1). A life, however, is to be judged by its fruits, by the attraction the soul experiences for divine things, by the aversion it feels for venial sin, by its progress in humility, self-denial, obedience, and love of God and neighbor. Some very imperfect souls, basing themselves on a false principle of quietude, sometimes believe that they are in such a state. They are only in a dangerous inertia. What do they do, and what can they possibly do that is good, if they can neither merit, nor practice virtue, nor increase it other than by acts? To prevent every illusion, then, we must meditate often on the true means to obtain this union.

Means to Obtain It

The means for obtaining this union are that which the Sacred Heart teaches us: "Learn from Me, for I am meek and humble of heart, and you will find rest for your souls." Our Lord is pleased to sum up in these two words, humility of heart and meekness, the whole Christian life and the whole of perfection.

There is a very profound reason for this: humility is the root of all Christian virtues, and meekness is its flower. Certainly charity is the highest virtue, the bond of perfection, and we ought to strive to nourish in ourselves its ardor, the zeal of charity. But, we must take care that our zeal, even though very ardent and intense, is humble and meek. Only then will we be saints. Humility produces in us an emptiness that God fills with Himself. Without humility the virtues are false virtues, exterior, pharisaic, hypocritical virtues, inspired by self-love and spiritual pride.

At the root of all virtues there ought to be humility: not only that humility which is exterior and formed with words, but humility of the heart; not a forced humility that comes from delusions, displeasures or the fear of not succeeding, but humility of the heart, willed for the love of God, born of the knowledge that God alone is great, while we are nothing. Our Lord surely does not love humility that is melancholy, sad, or of bad humor, urging us to set ourselves apart and to remain inactive. Rather, He loves that humility of heart that is happy to act and sacrifice self for God.

If humility is the principle of all virtues, meekness, according to the expression of St. Francis de Sales, is the flower of charity. In a plant the flower is the part most visible and beautiful because of the splendor and variety of its colors. It attracts with the perfume it releases. And despite its fragility and delicacy, its function is one of the most important in the plant because it protects and conserves the fruit. The same holds true for meekness in the case of charity. This is what is most visible and what attracts and entices us most to the practice of this great virtue. It is manifested in the smile, the glance, in one's bearing, in one's way of acting and in the choice of one's words; it doubles the value of service rendered.

Like the flower, it protects the fruit of charity leading us to accept counsels and reproaches alike. We may have the most ardent zeal for our neighbor, but yet, if we are not meek it seems that we do not love him, and we thus lose the fruit of our good intentions. Moreover, it will be impossible to resist certain difficulties that are frequently encountered in the practice of charity, because it is necessary to love not only those who are good and are pleasing to us, but also those whose company is wholly other than pleasing, a thing that becomes impossible without meekness. Clearly if humility and meekness are not to be only exterior virtues but rather virtues of the heart, if one is to be humble and meek not only in temperament but in supernatural virtue, and if one is to be such in relation to all, then a complete abnegation is required, a total abandonment to Providence.

If we wish to practice these virtues in the diverse circumstances of life, we must contemplate them often in our two great models: Our Lord and the Blessed Virgin. We ought to have an ardent devotion for the Blessed Virgin, the humble and meek Virgin Mary. The nineteenth century is said to be her century because of her most glorious apparitions and the definition of her Immaculate Conception. The twentieth century, which opened with the consecration of the human race to the Sacred Heart, seems to be the century of the Sacred Heart of Jesus. We should earnestly unite these two devotions as they will teach us the perfection of charity with humility and meekness.

Humility could not belong to Our Lord other than as man. It cannot be a divine virtue precisely because it is the expression of absolute dependence and submission of the creature to God. Humility signifies the abasement of the creature before God and before what is divine in others. Yet, no one better understood nor more desired this dependence and submission of his human nature than Our Lord. It is precisely He, the man greatest in mind and heart, who wishes to be the standard, the exemplar of humility: "Learn from Me for I am meek and humble of heart."

To make up for our pride and our rebellious wills, Our Lord abased Himself before His Father, accepting every kind of humiliation from His judges, from Pilate and from Herod. He voluntarily took the role of the representative of sinners, yet He was Sanctity itself. If we consider that sin debases human nature much lower than human nature itself, and even lower than nothingness, then no limits can describe the infinite self-annihilation of Christ. Comprehending the infinite gravity of sins which He assumed to Himself, He related them to the infinite grandeur of God, whose rights had been trampled upon and denied.

This humility that was so profound in Our Lord was at the same time a humility of the heart, simple as that of a child. When His disciples asked Him: "Who is the greatest in the King-dom of Heaven?" Jesus responded by calling a child and putting him in their midst. "I tell you solemnly, unless you change and become like little children you will never enter the Kingdom of Heaven. And so, the one who makes himself as little as this little child is the greatest in the Kingdom of Heaven" (Mt. 18:1–4).

The meekness of Our Lord is wholly supernatural. It derives from His zeal for the salvation of souls, and, far from diminishing His zeal, this meekness protects its fruits and guarantees its influence. Isaiah had announced Christ as the model of meekness: "Here is my servant whom I uphold, my chosen one in whom my soul delights. I have endowed him with my spirit that he may bring true justice to the nations. He does not cry or shout aloud, or make his voice heard in the streets. He does not break the crushed reed, nor quench the wavering flame. Faithfully he brings true justice; he will neither waver, nor be crushed until true justice is established on earth, for the islands are awaiting his law" (Isa. 42:1–4; cf. Mt. 12:18–21).

To St. Peter, Jesus replies that it is necessary to pardon not only seven times, but seventy times seven, that is, always. Jesus wished to be called the Lamb who takes away the sins of the world by His sacrifice because the lamb is a symbol of meekness: when it is immolated, it utters not a sound of lament. In His baptism, the Holy Spirit hovered above His head under the form of a dove, another symbol of meekness.

These two virtues, the germ and flower of all the others, are also found in their highest degree in Mary. She has been elevated above the angels because she is the model of humility. "He has looked upon His lowly handmaid. Yes, from this day forward all generations will call me blessed. . . .He has pulled down princes from their thrones, and exalted the lowly" (Lk. 1:48 and 52). Like her divine Son, she is an exemplar of meekness, as we sing every day in the *Salve Regina.*

The practice of these two virtues, united to a fervent daily Communion, will make charity, together with the gifts of the Holy Spirit and union with God, increase in us more every day. The sacrament of Love—the most excellent of all—is the sacrament of the most intimate union: it contains Jesus Christ in person, while the other sacraments contain only His supernatural power and are ordered to the Eucharist as to their end. Communion is, therefore, the most perfect act of the interior life, and if we prepare ourselves for it with humility, zeal, and meekness, we shall find there the most efficacious means for union with God. While our body receives the body of Christ, our soul is united to His soul, our intelligence to His light, our heart to the everburning sun of His love. Our Lord unites Himself to us to assimilate us to Himself, to make of us other Christs.

Every Communion that is not sacrilegious and sterile increases the degree of charity in us. Who then can measure the effects of daily Communion, above all of fervent daily Communion?

Conclusion

If in Holy Communion we learn meekness and humility from the divine Master, together with zeal for the glory of God and the salvation of souls, we will find refreshment for our souls according to Jesus' promise (Mt. 11:29). We will find an orderly peace and tranquility; we will realize a harmony of soul which, when fully subject to God, will receive His vivifying influence; there will be a harmony of body and soul, of the senses and the spirit. We will find peace and will be able to give it to others.

We should learn by experience. In a moment of disturbance and weariness, we ought to strive to practice humility and meekness; then we will notice how true the words of Our Lord are. We will find peace in loving. But we cannot obtain this peace in a stable manner without an unceasing war against ourselves, against the world, and against the Devil. It is for this reason that Jesus told us that He had come here below to bring the sword and war. How could one be meek and humble of heart with everyone without continually suffering violence, without pardoning others much, and without placing oneself lower than others?

Consequently, a war exists, but a war at the confines of the soul—if we can use this expression—while all within, the heart of the city and the fortress, is secure and remains tranquil, in peace and calm. "With God on our side who can be against us?" (Rom. 8:31). If I love God and if I think that God loves me, what does all the rest matter? This intimate peace gives abundant compensation for all the sacrifices it demands, and it is for this reason that Our Lord adds: "You will find rest for your souls. Yes, My yoke is easy and My burden light" (Mt. 11:29–30).

The Venerable Louis Bloy has left us a picture of the man who has attained this union and this peace. Among other things, he said: "God is often more pleased to dwell in the heart of one of these humble ones than in many other hearts that are not so intimately united to Him" (*De adhaerendo Deo*).

Lord, give us the zeal with which Your Sacred Heart burns; give us also a profound humility that makes us always adhere to You more while we become detached from ourselves; give us the meekness that will make souls accept what we say to them for the glory of Your Father and for their own salvation.

Grant us a more intimate union with your Sacred Heart present in the Eucharist, and guide us toward that wholly divine configuration that will make us Your brothers for eternity.

ONE YEAR.
20 MINUTES A DAY.

Encounter the Power and Wonder of God's Word with *Bible in a Year*. The simple format guides you through all 73 books of the Bible in just one year.

Learn more at **CatholicBibleInAYear.com**

What's the big deal about being Catholic? ▶

Unlock the Truth of your
Catholic Faith with a free
trial at **formed.org.**

FORMED®